NO SECOND PRIZE

written by Sean O'Tuathail
& illustrated by John Tohill

Published 2022
by John Tohill

ISBN 978-0-473-66105-2 (Paperback – printed)
ISBN 978-0-473-66806-8 (Paperback – print-on-demand)
ISBN 978-0-473-66106-9 (Epub)
ISBN 978-0-473-66107-6 (Kindle)

© Copyright 2022
All rights reserved.

Except for the purpose of fair reviewing, no part of this publication may be reproduced or transmitted in any form or by any means, electronic or mechanical, including photocopying, recording or any information storage and retrieval system, without prior written permission from the publisher.

Designed and distributed in New Zealand by
The Copy Press, Nelson, New Zealand.
www.copypress.co.nz

CONTENTS

Author's Note / vii

Disclaimer / ix

Foreword / x

Pocket Oxford / xii

PART ONE / 1
VARIOUS THOUGHTS PERTAINING TO THE HUMAN CONDITION

PART TWO / 45
POLITICS

PART THREE / 79
THE PUKEKO LIBERATION FRONT

PART FOUR / 95
THE SHEDS

PART FIVE / 105
FEMINISM

PART SIX / 117
SERVICE

PART SEVEN / 165
ADDICTION

PART EIGHT / 187
MENTAL HEALTH

PART NINE / 213
ROOTS

PART TEN / 235
FAITH

Appendix / 333

AUTHOR'S NOTE

This carefully crafted work is dedicated to all people experiencing "Bipolar Disorder." All I can say really is that I hope they get over the hurdles of the condition and get a life someday. Alexander the Great, Napoleon and Winston Churchill did, though I can't say which way they went in the end – up or down. There are many drugs and therapies available to the average Manic – depressive these days. None will work if said Manic – depressives don't want them to. That's the rub for wives, husbands, partners, children and friends. It's not an illness because it can't be fixed – it's a way of life. If you want to try and get into the mind of this particular Manic – depressive (and that's an open invitation to any shrinks out there), bearing in mind you may never get out, read on and find out what Manic – depression does!

    Content may puzzle, offend, or go right over the heads of some – maybe you belong in face book land. I don't give a flying Fernando because you are reading this now and maybe someone else will – that is my aim. The ironic thing about the following material is that ultra conservative religious cranks and other such people won't be happy with, and hopefully will be, challenged by my material. At least it's original which is more than I can say for theirs. And thus likewise by the same token liberal secular neo-pagans will also be challenged. I've found life's answers don't lie with any of these extremes. In fact if you have found the answer to life, the universe and everything give me a ring or send me an email. At one end of these poles you've got a downer and the other an upper – both result in despair and we can't have that. Can we?

    So stand in the middle and follow that straight ol' line.

    Postscript – one per cent of the population is Bi-polar

DISCLAIMER

Sean is the alter ego of John Tohill. He is the Author of the following collection and features in interviews with Dr Dick Shinnery of Ekatahuna University fame (among others) these important interviews are included in this work.

The opinions expressed in the following can in no way be attributed to Mr Tohill – they belong to Sean O'Tuathail.

Sean, unfortunately, has "Grumpy Old Man's Syndrome" at times is very politically incorrect. He thinks he can get away with it by hiding behind John who cops the inevitable flak. Without John, though, he wouldn't exist and he knows that.

John wishes to state that Sean is responsible for the following material although some of the drawings are signed by John. These were done before Sean started taking him over and emerging in a mainly literary form.

John worries about having a split personality but Sean only manifests on paper. This masterpiece does not claim to be about Manic – depression, it is only dedicated to those movers and shakers who have the condition. Manic depression is an experience thing.

Religion is mentioned. Sean claims that Jesus is his best mate, so does John. After all, Jesus said that His followers are His friends – even if they drink beer.

Sean also writes from a South Island, New Zealand "working class man" perspective and makes no apologies for that.

Sean and John – or is it John and Sean? – invite readers to tear their eyes away from twitter and face book and pick up a good dictionary to look up the meanings of the words "metaphor, analogy, sarcasm" and of course "irony" (this will help) and read on.

The drawings included mostly are not related to the writings but the symbolism in some may go a long with some of the written material.

FOREWORD

By professor Dick Shinnary, head of Linguistics and Logical Positivism Departments, Ekatahuna University.

The following contains what could be to some people moderately offensive material. The content hereinafter is abbreviated or written "shorthand", because Sean knows from experience that one cannot tell a long story to people with short attention spans. Anyway, I'll keep this short because I've got to shoot off across the ditch to Wagga Wagga University to present a lecture on closer linguistic relations with my Australian counterparts. Getting back to it, Sean's masterpiece, I'd like to suggest that if you are not P.C. and it's not computers I'm talking about – although some reading this might need information punched into them – and you haven't got an attention deficit disorder, dyslexic problems and you drink lots of beer, you might read this stuff and have a wee think. You can read between the lines if you like. You might even get something out of it – even if you are out of it.

    There are not a few allusions to Jesus, who Sean says is his Saviour and a bit of other associated material. Sean likes Jesus and considers Him his best mate and if you like Jesus too you may well concur with Sean. Sean hopes the following will challenge you to get out of the cosy little world you live in and take up your cross as it were. He certainly has challenged me. I'm off to Wagga Wagga to immerse myself into Intellectualism!

    If you really don't like the following material, then in the interests of sustainability you can use it as toilet paper or perhaps put it in your worm farm. Be sure to tear the pages up into little strips to facilitate easier breakdown by the worms. Failing this method of disposal put the material in your paper recycling bin ensuring you put it out for collection on the correct week. Remember it's glass one week, and paper etc on the alternate week. Sean tells me he got this mixed up a couple of times and ended up with an embarrassing amount of empty beer bottles to put out. If in doubt, ring or email your local council – they are always happy to help with your enquiries. Sean assures me no animals have been hurt in the course of compiling this work, except of course the animals that had to die previous to Sean's downtrodden ex-wife cooking bits of them for his tea.

Some people may need to a dictionary as a companion to reading the verbosity contained in this work. There are some big multi-syllable words that may be a challenge to some, but Sean has kept them to a minimum. There are some excerpts from the Catechism of the Catholic Church and the Jerusalem Bible, so don't attack Sean for anything said – blame God.

I can hopefully say that Protestant Fundamentalists, crazy Charismatic's, woolly thinking liberals and stiff necked Catholic "conservatives" may not like the material contained here on in. Sean hopes so – because that's why he compiled it. Sean reckons these people have for far too long locked Jesus up in a safe thereby making Him inaccessible to the average punter. They think they are the only ones with the combination. Sean has also included some original pictorial material not only to confound the people that can read but to give people that can't something to look at. Sean would like to thank his dog, Tess who apparently protects his shed – where he writes and draws all this bizarre stuff – from cats who would probably piss all over everything if she wasn't in there sleeping. A special mention might be made here to Barbara, Sean's ex-wife, who used to cook his tea.

Editorial note – Dr Dick likes to write in long paragraphs because he is an Academic.

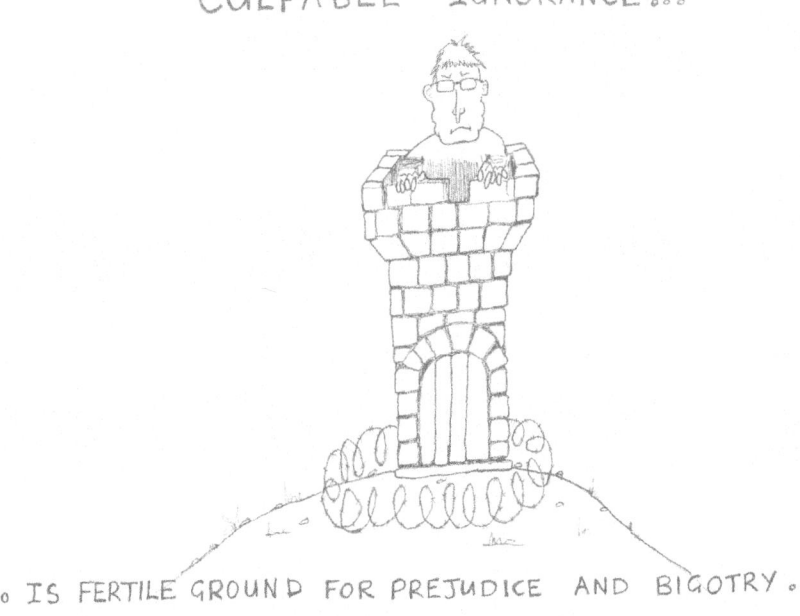

CULPABLE IGNORANCE...

... IS FERTILE GROUND FOR PREJUDICE AND BIGOTRY.

POCKET OXFORD

Pride: A feeling of honour and self-respect.

A sense of self growth.

Courage.

Spirit.

Self-respect due to the avoidance of unworthy actions.

Courage: The power or quality of dealing with or facing danger, fear or pain.

The freedom from fear or its disturbing effects.

Spirit: The basic emotional and activating principle of a person "will".

An emotional state especially with regard to exaltation or dejection.

The element in man regarded as separable from and animating the body of a person from the intellectual, moral or emotional point of view.

Life force Something that drives a man aside from his mental, physical and emotional being (Chi).

Arrogant: Having or showing an exaggerated opinion of one's own importance, merit, ability, etc.

Cowardice: Lack of courage in facing danger, pain or difficulty.

False pride: Tendency to avoid as degrading what is not so.

Excessive self-esteem, conceit.

Ego: One's image of oneself, morale.

Conceit.

Self-centredness.

Soul: The spirit or immaterial part of man, the seat of human personality, intellect, will and emotions; regarded as an entity that survives the body after death.

The spiritual part of a person capable of redemption from sin through divine grace.

The immaterial part of man regarded as immortal or as subject to salvation and damnation or as animating the body or as existing independently of it or as the true self or as the organ of emotion and thought and will (Human Being).

Humility: The state or quality of being humble.

Conscious of one's failings, unpretentious.

Dignity: The state or quality of being.

Worthy of honour.

My Words: All the above aspects of a human being are interrelated like a big ball of spaghetti. Damage one aspect and it affects the others.

Sean O'Tuathail
For Dr Dick Shinnery

PART I
VARIOUS THOUGHTS PERTAINING TO ...

...THE HUMAN CONDITION

THE END

The Thrush awoke before dawn,
He put his feathers on,
And took a beak from the Ancient Gallery,
He had a bit of a chirp.
And he flew down off his tree,
And landed deftly on the lawn.
And he searched there for a worm,
He found one and ate it.
And he hopped on around for a while,
He came across a stroppy Blackbird,
And he hopped off and ate another worm.
He then came across some Sparrows,
And he ate another worm.
He got chased by a big Tui,
Then he hopped up onto the deck,
And looked around for a while......
....Then he saw the cat,
He flew off in a great panic,
Straight into the ranch slider window
That's it – the End.

P.S. the moral of this story is …… If you live by the beak, you'll die by the beak.

THE ANSWER

"Well, Mr Tryingtogetaheadavitch, pursuant to said clauses appropriate to the subsection 5 of the amended recent legislation and in view of current statistical trends and our experts anecdotal observations and funding being channelled to more pressing areas such as grants for one armed Eskimo Lesbian University lecturers and their significant others, as well as funding also being redirected to battle the continued and persistent assault by objective truth on our ideologically dynamic proactive relativistic institutions, there is not much money left to fund your fact finding task force. So, in short, the answer to your request is not quite as straight forward at this present point in time, but going forward and, in light of a projected fiscal update in the upcoming financial year, we may want to look at the situation again, in the meantime, if you fill out Form 0; FOUR ONE and NOUGHT; E; as well as Form F.A.R.; Q we will consider your application."

I AM THE CREEPY FUCKER THAT HAUNTS YOU IN YOUR DREAMS OR MAYBE YOU HAVE AN' APPOINTMENT WITH ME AT SOME OFFICE OF A GOVERNMENT DEPARTMENT.

INTERRUPTUS MAXIMUS – A SUNDAY EXPERIENCE

Its Sunday afternoon, worked on nightclub door last night
There's a knock on the door, I open it to see a suit and a tie
Complete with briefcase and woman in tow.
I say "g'day".
He smiles falsely and reaches into his case
He pulls out his religious tract
Like a Real Estate salesman with a contract.
The woman smirks looking me up and down
A prim vulture, she already has me pigeonholed
Staring at my tight jeans, hedonist t-shirt and long hair.
I wonder what she was like before her conversion.
Still the same, by the look in her eyes.

The salesman flashes this pamphlet in my face
Complete with pictures of the promised world to come
The people pictured all seem to have short back and sides,
Their women are ugly, you have to wear a suit and tie!
He says, "We have come to show you the promised land!"
Tersely I inquire, "Who are you?"
Looking her in the eye.
She smiles dazzlingly, "Jehovah's Witnesses", says he
Somewhat sheepishly.

"Baaaaa" is what I want to say,
They can't even spell God's name right!
"I am Catholic", I say instead.
Oh, you'll have respect for the Bible then".
"Just God; The Father, Son and Holy Spirit", say I.
"Oh" shock was evident on his face
The Bible being rummaged for was returned
She gives a self-righteous look
"See ya later", I say.
They scuttle off at a loss for words
    Obviously only a few were needed from me.
I shut the door with a grin

Intending to write the experience down
Which I am doing right now.

Just imagine if we turned up at their place
At six AM on a Monday morning
Swinging on the end of a bottle of Tullamore Dew,
The missus with a slab of stubbies under her arm
Her chewing PK, smoking a joint, resplendent low cut slip
Professing to be devout pissed up Testicosticals
Saying that we had been given a tip
That this was the Archangel Michael's pad
And he was throwing a party, letting it rip
The end was imminent and it was party time.
See, I could shove my life down their throat too
But there are many paths, towards that final destination
Just be sure yours doesn't go over a cliff
The vehicle you use is up to you
Be a Chevy, a Harley, a Morrie or Ford
Just watch out for the flashy salesman
Who tries to sell you a Jap import
Fantastic on the broad highway
Not much good on the gravel road.

PS What do you call a deer with no eyes?
Answer: No eye deer.

Apologies Kevin Bloody Wilson

ONE LINERS – PHILOSOPHICAL TRASHCAN

1. Wisdom doesn't come with age
   Enlightenment doesn't come with knowledge
   Intelligence doesn't come with information
   Learning doesn't come from school
   Listening doesn't come from hearing
   Heeding doesn't come from advice
   Seeing doesn't come from looking
   Truth doesn't come from facts

2. Sin doesn't come from temptation
   Preachers don't always come from God
   Faith doesn't come from religion
   Bravery can only come from faith
   Christianity isn't coming from all churches
   The spirit doesn't come from ink and paper
   Love doesn't come from sex

3. Freedom doesn't come from democracy
   Happiness doesn't come from having
   Peace doesn't come from ceasefire
   Dignity doesn't come from winning
   Humility doesn't come from apology

4. Racism doesn't come from colour
   Wealth doesn't come from money
   Aristocracy doesn't come from superiority
   Estate doesn't come from acquisition
   Discernment doesn't come from privilege
   Victory doesn't come from destruction
   Conquest doesn't come from subjugation
   And justice definitely doesn't come from the law

5. So where the hell are you coming from?
   Aye!

WUHAN TAKEAWAYS

JUST BACK FROM THE WUHAN MARKET...

... A WALK BEFORE DINNER

HEAVEN ON THE TAKAKA HILL

0530
I woke up and had a cup of tea
And listened to the bellbird chorus
Stuck some porridge on the stove
I stared into space and dreamed a bit
Said some prayers and read a bit of my Bible
Then I smoked a cigarette
Looked at the trees swaying in the breeze
I ate my porridge and put on some coffee
Drank that with another smoke.

I gave the dog a pat
Which gave me an idea
We get into the ute and drive to the track
We get out and start climbing
Tess scouting ahead
Beech forest mingled with karst landscape
Amazing views, this is cool
The dog thinks the smells are cool too
Suddenly we see feral goats
Tess gives chase, barking her head off
After a while she returns,
Catching up with me.

Back to the ute and we drive home
On arrival Tess sees a rabbit
And she gives chase
She gives up
I give her a pat
And the consolation prize of a Smacko.

I have a cup of tea
And go and do some jobs for my wife
Later I have some beers
And digest the day
We have dinner and watch some TV
I'm tired so I go to bed
(Should have taken the rifle)

GLUTEN FREE

We want to be:

Mortgage free; Gluten free; Positive; Dynamic; Vegetarian; Free range; Culturally sensitive; Multi cultural; Spiritually alternative; Politically correct; Reproductively healthy; Nut allergy aware; Gender neutral; safe; Smoke free; Non-judgmental; Tolerant; Progressive, conservatively liberal, liberally conservative; Centralist left leaning while being to the right of too far to the left of being out there – somewhere; Fat free; Cyclist friendly with complete access for pedestrians including mobility scooters, respectful of stork and disabled car parking spaces; sensitive to our pets varied dietary needs; Respectful of the Tangata Whenua and other minorities especially staff at WINZ considering unemployment is rising; respectful of the Treaty of Waitangi; Using less salt in our diet; exercising more; drinking less beer; driving less aggressively; being more sustainable; burning less fossil fuels; giving strangers spontaneous hugs; carrying out random acts of kindness; Being more aware of climate change (in some cases – experts); kinder to small animals, little children, Canadians and economists; kinder to senior citizens escaping from their retirement gulags on stolen mobility scooters; being serious about wearing high vis vests at all times so we can be seen in public and be safe from big truck drivers; Saving the environment from plastic bags and third world over population; opening more wellness centres with vibrating massage chairs and colonic therapy facilities; centering our Chakras and cleansing our auras; being more kind to EMOs and Marilyn Manson devotees; more sensitive to Boy Racer needs; Watching re runs of Australian Master Chef for continued inspirational well-being (along with Marlborough wine); trying recipes from the Christchurch Press; and of course, using Viagra ™.

RICHARD CRANIUM HAD ONLY JUST STEPPED BACK ONTO THE DIAS AND HE WAS LODGING A PROTEST AS HE HAD BEEN RELEGATED TO SECOND PLACE FOR LOOKING FIRST PRIZE IN THE MOUTH.

Apologies Winchester

SOUTHERN MAN – AN INTROSPECTIVE DISSERTATION

I'm from south of the Waitaki
Where men are men and sheep are scared
Apparently our drink is Speights,
Not too much or you'll lose your mates.
MAY THE ROAD RISE UP TO MEET YOU.

I don't know why I think like I do,
But really, a spade is always a spade.
Talk shorthand and think in pictures
I can't help it, that's how I am made.
MAY THE WIND BE ALWAYS AT YOUR BACK.

Just want to work for a fair day's pay,
But the bosses get richer and promise the sky.
Is this the only way?
You ask the question "why?"
MAY THE SUN SHINE WARM ON YOUR FACE.

Been here and there, paid my dues,
Seen those flying pigs in Wellington.
Can't make much sense of the news
Same old pendulum swinging.
MAY THE RAINS FALL SOFT ON YOUR FIELDS.

Got to accept what comes my way
No point in crying over spilt milk.
Never mind, always another day
That's the point, Our day will come.
AND UNTIL WE MEET AGAIN........

......MAY GOD HOLD YOU IN THE PALM OF HIS HAND

FARNARCLE

The following are extracts from an interview with Dr Dick Shinnery, Professor of Linguistics and Logical Positivism at Ekatahuna University. He is previously of a prestigious Gore establishment.

The subject of this interview is the word F***. I have censored the word here by using an F and three asterisks. I have used this word many times myself in uncensored form, probably a couple of hundred thousand times by now. As a Catholic, I know swearing is a venial sin and doing so can incur many years in purgatory, so I cannot encourage others to do the same.

And of course some of my Evangelical Protestant friends would say that by using the word like I do, I was never really a Christian and I'm going to hell.

Interview:

"Dr Dick, what are the origins of the word in question?"

"Well Sean, the word has evolved into its present form from the ancient term, "farnarcle" often used by defeated combatants such as the Welsh, Irish, Scots and French in their wars against the English. This might possibly explain the phrase 'Excuse my French.' The emotions preceding this expression are still present today, hence the endurance of the term. A way to describe the emotion would be when, say you are caught down a blind alley and there's no way out and three or four large (possibly dark) gentlemen are approaching you exhibiting a rather menacing demeanour. At this point – according to research – most people would utter the expletive in question. And I think Sean there may be a special dispensation from your Church for saying F*** in this case."

"Ah. That's nice to know Dr Dick, but what is the meaning of the word today in particular?"

"Well Sean, as you know you can pick up an Oxford or Collins dictionary today and find that some English wankers have decided it's a taboo word and it's all about bonking, the buggers are sex mad. But I hope to explain to you during the course of this interview, using the Kiwi vernacular – an ancient and noble language free from Pommy colloquialisms – employing technical terms developed at Gore and Ekatahuna Universities, the linguistic applications of this much maligned word."

"Carry on, Dr Dick."

"F*** is perhaps the most versatile word in the Kiwi language and we used it in a most unique way, particularly for those who wish to revert to "talking shorthand."

"Some examples of the use of the word in our vernacular are:
"We had a f***in huar (another versatile but less taboo expletive) of a party."

Translation – I've got a hangover.

"Jeez, that was a f***en good try" – Rugby or League.

"Dirty f***er" – many applications.

"F***en cold (or hot)" – the weather.

"F*** you" – singular expletive.

"F*** them" – a wider application.

"F*** the lot of you" – spoken from an isolated perspective.

"F*** that" – not into that.

"F*** off" – self explanatory.

"F*** me" – an expression of bemusement.

"F*** all that" – an expression of disgust immediately preceding going and getting pissed immortalised in song by the great Kiwi band Pink Floyd.

"Do I look like I give a F***?" – expression of disinterest.

"Can't be f***ed" – expression of Fatigue.

"The country's f***ed" – a "shorthand" way of explaining the current Account deficit, the GDP, Exports, the fiscal situation and the general moral decline.

"This is a real clusterf***." – a military term used by Junior officers or platoon commanders facing multiple problems in the heat of battle.

"F***" – generic term.

"These are some of the more common uses of the term, Sean; I see it being used a lot more considering the state of the country at the moment."

"I see. How do you see the word benefiting our nation now and looking forward?"

"Well, environmentally speaking I think more use of the term in spoken form would be far more sustainable in terms of… "Can I have another beer, Sean?"

"Here you go, Dr Dick."

"Thanks, now where was I? Oh yeah, Global Warming is upon us (although Gore University experts aren't sure) because of increased CO_2 emissions, right?"

"Go on, Dr Dick"

"When a person talks a lot he, or particularly she, emits excess carbon dioxide, right?"

"Well, I suppose so."

"Well, when you use the F word and other expletives you cut down on the amount of verbiage you use, hence economy of speech and less carbon dioxide emissions. For example – "F*** this beer tastes good!" Far simpler than going into a long winded wine wanker type dissertation on the brewing process and the geographical origins of the hops. Do you follow?"

"Well, yeah, here's another beer."

"Sean, a study commissioned by my colleagues at Ekatahuna University has shown there are huge amounts of CO_2 around Wellington – you can't blame the cows for that. People are saying it's a conspiracy by the Politicians. What they have found is that if the Politicians are found to be the cause of the problem, the people might demand they pay a CO_2 tax thus negating further pay rises."

"Is that right, Dr Dick?"

"The studies have been done, Sean. Look, if people thought before they spoke, relaxed and had a few beers – not wine it makes you uptight and anally retentive – and judiciously used F words instead of dribbling lots of P.C. crap all the time we'd cut down on CO_2 emissions hugely. The only drawback is there would be an increase in the number of people feeling offended and needing counselling. But hey, we're talking the future of the planet here, Sean"

"I think I'll have another beer. Would you like one Dr Dick?"

"Ta, Sean."

"What about the use of the F word in its written form?"

"Same thing, but in applying the F word in its written form, we'd save our forests by using less paper."

"Go on."

"Just imagine how much better it would be if we didn't have to pay bureaucrats and private sector paper pushers to compose lengthy documents concerning policy and all that other stuff. I mean, you go into a Govt department building these days and you can just see the trees getting chopped down. There's more paper getting fired about now than there ever was despite the advent of computers. And it's shiny expensive shit too, Sean."

"Just think how much simpler the Health and Safety act could be with the word F***wit inserted in the appropriate places. This, I would say, to be much more cost effective."

"Then imagine written replies from MSD, ACC and the IRD such as "Not f***en likely", No f***ken way." And "f*** off."

"Things would be so much simpler and less stressful Sean."

"I'm beginning to see your point Dr Dick, f*** it let's have another beer."

"F***en good idea, Sean!"

TICKER

Beat the clock manage your time
Must get the work completed
Before you hear the bells of hell chime
Break new records
Race against the watch
Be a hero for a fleeting moment
Make history and feel so sublime

Scurrying like two legged ants
Going about futile endeavours
Smart arses, time and motion honing
What a waste of precious life
So addicted they are
Soldiering on with flu capsules

One doing the job of two
Dreaming of those elusive two weeks
In Bali drinking foreign beer
Getting burnt in a warmer clime
What a way to piss away time

Meanwhile the boss rakes it in
You have a stroke or heart attack
Your missus takes up Prozac
And finally buggars off
With your best mate, she feels scorned
Should have given her more and kept her warm

Save five minutes, take a short cut
Can't be late for gym class
So you fuck the job up and must do it again
Because you're worried about sagging bust or arse
Why bother when we all suffer those ravages
Of time and gravity

Well time's near up clever dick
With your nest egg you plan to retire

But to your dismay you'll find
Those rats and moths have chewed your pile
So it's the Super pension
Now that will cramp your style
You turn to your man made church
All bitter and full of bile

You may be wholly unaware
But the ol' "Fig Tree" is nearly ripe
Why do you put your faith in Viagra
And the surgeon's steely knife?
Now the genetic engineer has reared his unspeakable head
You'll sell to any nasty bloke
Your fat arse just for one last breath
You never believed that anyone
But you was master of your fate
Sorry Bud, it's too fucking late

You would never understand the reason
Why you've been allowed to live so long
Someone was giving you time
To undo all you're wrongs
And to grasp the True meaning
Behind the 16th century language
In that Book you so diligently read
Not knowing that every time you thumped it
And did vindictively point
There were three fingers of your own
Pointing back at you

Maybe your Grandkids will find the Way
And not give a shit for the cares
Of this mad and bloody world of Today
But the value of each sunrise
And its promise of a good day

The ticking of the Universal Clock
Its not ours to buy or quantify
Go and live life to the full

Live in Truth and not the Lie
Don't hurt your neighbour either

Time is not a tool of your will
Remember, that next tick
Just might be your last
Your very own Omega you silly prick
I hope like me you had a blast
Tomorrow is coming fast!

Yee Haa!

THEY HADN'T PICKED IT UP YET BUT THERE WAS A SLIGHT MALFUNCTION IN THE TIME AND MOTION MACHINE.

THE NEWS TODAY – 2009

North Korea let off another bomb
Billy the hunted got caught
Some paedophile is living next to a kindergarten
The Chinese brought some of F and P
Obama appointed some minority person to a post
The weather will be fine tomorrow
Lots of Brit MP's are set to resign
A Catholic got murdered by Prods in the six counties
Everyone has forgotten about Christine Rankin
Same old thing in the Holy Land
Everybody will forget about the swine flu too.
Maybe that's why they put the paedophile story in
Boy racers will have their cars crushed apparently
Karen Olsen's dress was nice tonight
John Key said "actually" a lot
I forgot what he was being interviewed for
Close up will be on soon with more infotainment
Coro streets on tonight – or is it?
I'm none the wiser
Shock horror, what year is it?

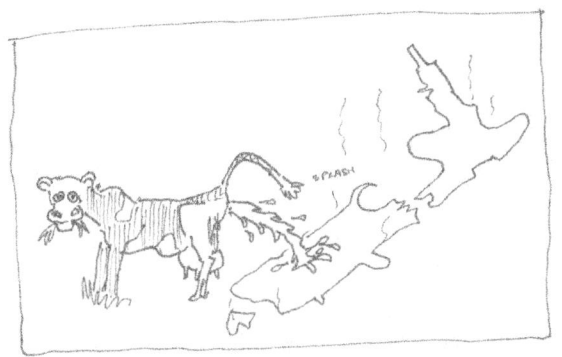

DON

The following are highlights from an interview with Professor Doner el Kebab, Head of Middle Eastern Studies at the University of Wagga Wagga during his recent visit to this country.

"Thank you for your time, Professor el Kebab".

"Not at all, Sean, call me Don".

"Let's get right to it, Don. What are the ways Australian, and to a lesser extent, New Zealand people, could be more welcoming and tolerant of immigrants and refugees from Islamic countries?"

"Well, Sean, when they get off the plane or are stuck in some refugee camp in the outback, they get very disorientated. I, and members of the Fair Dinkum Aussie Islamic Association, have put a proposal before the Federal Government that in order for our people to know where Mecca is, arrows pointing to there should be painted at key areas, such as railway stations, main roads etc".

"Do you think the size of the Islamic population warrants it?"

"Oh yes, Sean. There are so many Muslims in Sydney now the FDAIA is in negotiation with Saudi Arabian banks to finance us so we can buy the Centre Point tower and turn it into a minaret to call the faithful from as far as Parramatta and Western suburbs to prayer five times a day".

"Really?"

"Yes. And not only that, the revolving restaurant will be converted to a revolving mosque!"

"Don't you think there would be a problem with the worshipper's sense of direction?"

"Revolving arrows, Sean" always pointing to Mecca".

"I see. Everybody knows the Jews own Bondi. Do you see that being a problem in the future, considering the projected increase in the Muslim population?"

"Simple, Sean. We'll build a concrete wall around Bondi and put checkpoints at King's Cross Station and key roads going in."

"Don't you think that would be importing ancient enmities, Don?"

"Not at all. That's all lies propagated by Mossad and their Crusader allies, the CIA. The Jews think they were there first so we would only be accommodating their delusion in the interest of peace, which after all, is the definition of Islam."

"Ok, Well, what about the bad press taxi drivers from your part of the world are getting here in New Zealand?"

"From what I hear, the case you are alluding to there was some sort of cultural misunderstanding. They were only trying to be friendly. You have no idea what it does to an Afghan man when he sees a woman without a burkha. And if you are making accusations about Muslim taxi drivers over charging, I curse you and may the fleas and tics, yes tics, of a thousand million camels infest you and all the infidel journalist's armpits for a thousand generations!! Y@!"

"Would you like a cup of sweet tea, Don?"

"Oh yes thank you, it's just the Jews and CIA, they make me so mad."

"Well Don, I'd like to broach another touchy subject if you don't mind?"

"Yes"

"What are your views on the Somali woman hijacker and her antics recently?"

"Oh that's New Zealand's biggest problem, Sean."

"How's that, Don?"

"In New Zealand women get far too much freedom."

"Go on."

"Where I come from, we keep them behind walls and when they do go out they've got to wear burkhas. And we keep them worn out from having children so they haven't got time to be menstrual and cause havoc."

"That sounds a bit barbaric!"

"Not at all. We practise polygamy too so if one wife pisses you off, you favour one of the others – divide and rule – bingo; peace and happiness. Bloody expensive though."

"Sorry Don I think I may have given you my whiskey and ginger ale."

"That's the price you pay for freedom, Sean, the truth comes out. Can I have another one?"

"Here you go."

"Thanks"

"Tell me, Don, if we Christians, and your lot and the Jews and even the Buddhists and Hindus believe in the same God, why is there so much strife between us?"

"What religion are you, Sean?"

"Catholic, Don"

"Haven't you seen the Da Vinci Code? Catholics are just a secret society controlled by Opus Dei who are a branch of the CIA, a bunch of

Crusader infidel bastards financed by the Jewish Zionist Rockefellers and Rothschilds."

"But you guys are financed by the Saudi Arabians."

"So? Gis another whiskey and ginger ale."

"So what's the difference?"

"We, Sean" – gulp – "we believe in "Al Jezeera" or "Al" for short and he was put there by Ishmael centuries ago AND Sean, he got it from some alien shapeshifting Freemasons, way before the Cabal and those dickhead Templars mind you – the outfit that built the pyramids and Stonehenge. How can you stupid infidels not believe that? And Jesus was born under a palm tree, how can you believe all that manger bullshit? Apostasy right from the start!"

"That's interesting, Don. Maybe Christians and true believers have a wee way to go before they reach an understanding."

"Not at all, Sean, we are committed to fighting for peace with Christians wherever we are, after all that's what Islam means – peace. Don't you understand?"

"Well Don, there are many ex Christians here in the West who will welcome you, they are very tolerant you know."

"That's what we are counting on, Sean."

"Well, Don, where do you go from here?"

"I've decided to move to New Zealand – maybe Auckland or New Plymouth and get a job as a taxi driver."

"Why, Don."

"I hear there's a job coming at Massey University for a post graduate fellowship at the Religious Studies Faculty."

"You'll do well, Don, if you get the job!"

24 May 2009

AMERICA

We don't buy much from the US of A anymore
Yet they've kept nasty nigel from our shores
For quite a while now, some say.
The best and worst comes out of America
From Zippo lighters, Colt and Chevrolet
To Barack Obama and Opra Winfrey
We speak the same language, even if they can't spell
They kicked arse in Afghanistan for us, and Vietnam
And are sending the Taliban to hell, now ISIS

Everything we could want comes from America
Morally speaking we've all we need from them too
Beamed by satellite like a fast food spirituality
Creflo A Dolar, Robert Sheuller, and Jimmy Swaggart
Then there's the Fox Network and CNN
Making us feel secure and in the Right
Because there's big bad bogies out there
Just waiting to destroy our way of life
Why don't we buy much from the US anymore?

We should buy more from America
It only takes a bit of self discipline
To ignore the cheap stuff flooding our markets
From Pakistan, Vietnam, India and China
And drinking fair trade coffee. What's with that?
That's only helping America's evil enemies
We should support American products
Like cluster bombs, MacDonalds and light armoured vehicles
Because this will bring peace and prosperity to the world.

After all, that's what Barack Obama and his predecessors want
And that's peace in our time and freedom
Freedom to exploit the world and impose the American Way
If only we would buy more U.S. products
When are we going learn?
There are a few problems with that though

Like if all the Ponsonby Poofters bought Humvees
Motorways and carparks would have to be widened
This would make Auckland even bigger.

That would be like having a little bit of America here
And Auckland has been exploiting us for far too long
Bugger Wellington, the Jaffas are even worse
And me being from down South
I'd have to get the Rebel flag out along with my mates
This could start a civil war – here in Godzone
We don't want carpet baggers down here
No way, man
I can wear my Chinese made Swandri with a clear conscience

Now the Chinese, they're another story
AND THERE'S A LOT OF THEM IN AUCKLAND!

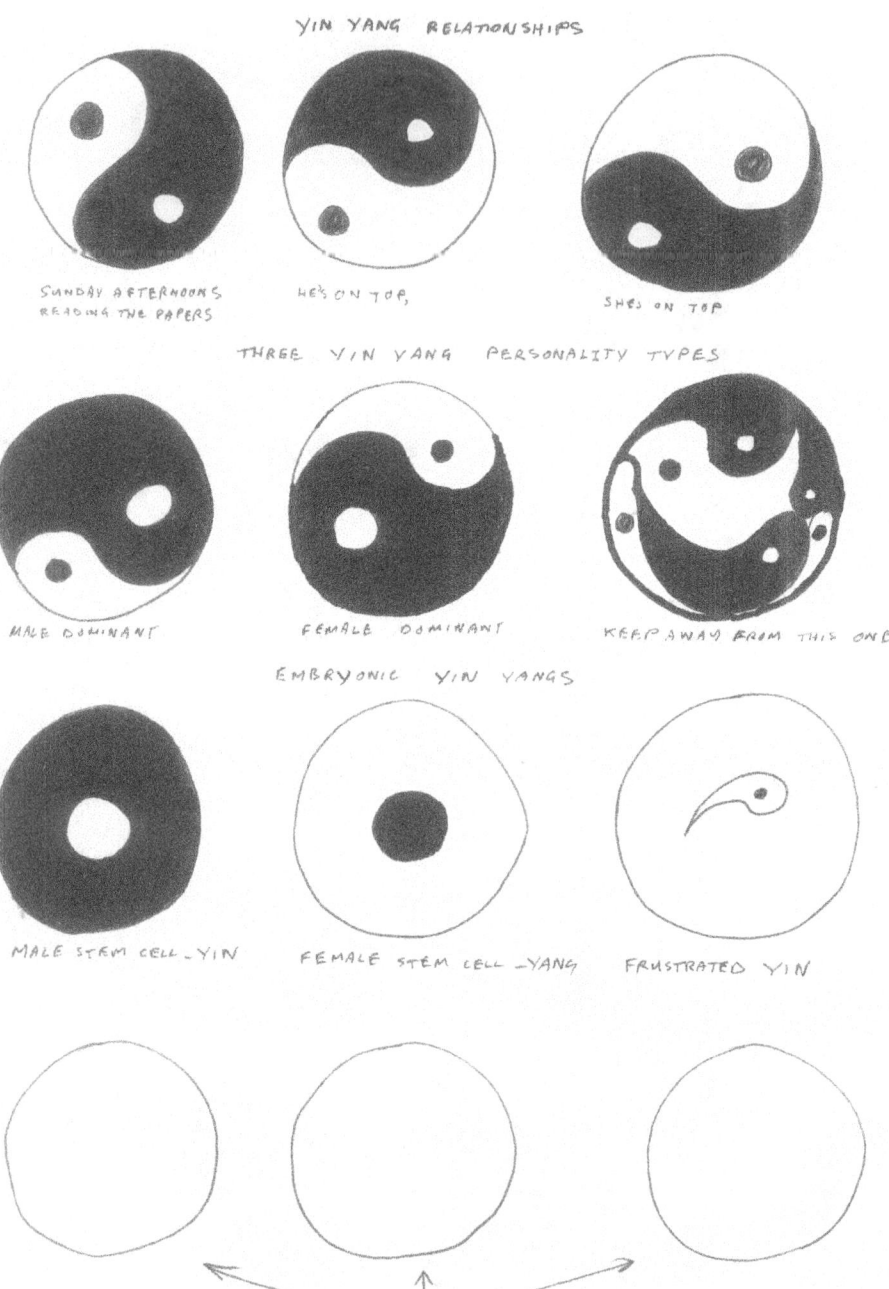

TWO OR THREE JO(H)NNY'S
(The explicated version!)

I was told once for no price
By a friend I have for life
Jim the Eagle is his name
This he said to me, in light bulb fashion
Amid his usual monologue rave
"A true man stands alone".
This was a great pearl to me he gave
I knew from life's lessons he was right
Just needed to hear it from a "brother".
They are the very words you see
That gives "Poltroons" an amount of bother
For meaning look up your dictionary.

The fact that I alone stand guard
At nightclub door, this very moment
Makes me a bit that way sometimes too
Right now my buddy, has gone round and through
Slipping in the door that leads out
In order to unobtrusively scout
The standard of punters mean
To make sure none are venting spleen
And he will be in no doubt
That for a blind spot of few seconds
He will be quite alone too!

Two or three hundred liquored units
In all varied degrees
Packed dance floor, deejay ministering
A queue at the bar and queue to do weez
Mostly nice people I spose
In their own sheep-like ways
Most we draft at the gate
A few goats and the odd silly lout
Still slip even attentive eye

But no mongrel dogs are about
Not inside our club anyway!!!

Hey, I spoke too soon, what's this?
Coming "staunch" up our strip
Red and Black demons, rather Hyena like
Complete with mile wide yellow streak
Looks like me and door handle again
"Such is life," Ned Kelly said.

I hope my back watcher, inside on standing patrol
Doesn't get held up too long in there
"One on one, but two deal with many".
Here they come, full of shit to the chin
Gabbling idiot dog soldier creed
The maggot fuckwits can never win
They steal, having no brains to build
Destined for D Block and/or the Bin
All I can do is stand my ground
If they take a penny, we'll eventually take a pound.

So I shut the door and say, so polite:
"No you may not pass around me or come in tonight"
Looking in these inbred "Rotties" right in the eyes
I feel like a wee "Border Collie" out on a crag
Waiting for movement through "one eighty sight".
No Mickey Mouse Thirteens will get in tonight
We don't mind going down in a fight
What do they do? Full stubbies, hidden tools and all
    They try to save face, without fight they retreat.

I ask me, I ask myself, I ask I
What the Hell, why stand for a lie?!!!!!

Jonni Wonni comes through the door
Turn around and through complete
"Or right?" he asks with tooth missing grin
I point with forehead at threat receding down street

"Didn't ya let 'em in?" says he
"Nah" says I, taken slightly aback.
"Cuppla coffees then?" says the fake cockney
"I reckon", I say lighting smokes with a shake.
It'll be "Buffalo Soldiers" next week
The thought emerges unbidden.

The Boss, God love him, complete with shaved pate
Comes bursting out, with authority to stamp.
He notes the appearance
Of the "silly lout" known to us so well
"Beanpole" is one of his many names.
We get a lecture on the evils; of coffee drinking,
Clocking too early, other numerous misdemeanours,
Far too numerous to have room to mention.
Buggery Bollocks really, due to the fact;
That I am still bloody shaking
Does he know the risks we are taking?
We are paid a "princely" sum
Compensation for loss of weekend
Can't be bothered to tell him
Not here for money, it's become an addiction.

A few minutes later or thereabouts
Legs up to there, miniskirt and with hair bleached
Airhead asks in high pitched screech
Boyfriend giggles worse than her, he's on a promise
"ARE YOU THE DOORMAN?" she's screaming in my ear.
I think of a use for the toe of my shoe.
A shit eating grin spreads across my face.
"YOU DON"T LOOK LIKE ONE" she screams louder
Boyfriend guffaws as though on cue.
Jonsky chokes on his flat white
He gives me that look of woe
A special doorman one, you know
"What fucking planet are they from?"
Is the question so often wordlessly passed.

You gotta love them,
You don't have to like them,
Most are born to be hunted and killed
Just look up Peter and revelation!

You, me, us and them
Through and Around, Around and Through
Eject nicely, before the buggers spew
"Have gun, will travel" a saying not new
Treat them well, right from the start
Blessed are the meek and mild at heart
For they shall have the door opened for them.
And from their money they will part
We win their hearts and minds
But always have zippo at the ready
To light the ol' metaphoric fuse
And blow their huts apart.
Never judge a cover by its book,
Or a book by its cover.

1545 30th June 1998

THEY FLIGHT TESTED THE PEAGLE, MUCH TO THE BEMUSEMENT OF THE ANCIENTS.

GETTING THE NUMBERS RIGHT ... OVERNIGHT

Part One:

Excerpts, official and unofficial, of an interview with Health Minister, Tony Ryall, who is rumoured to use facial exfoliants and regularly has a body wax.

News: 9 May 2009

"Mr Ryall said, the previous Government left him with 13 health priorities, 61 objectives, 10 health targets measured through 18 indicators, 25 other indicators of DHB performance and 4 hospital benchmark indicators assessed through 15 measures."

"We've had too many indicators and committees and targets for the last 9 years," he said.

The following are off the record comments made by someone sounding like Mr Ryall obtained from protected sources at Bellamys (The Barperson/man)

"...So we're going to reduce all those numbers down to a fiscally acceptable (burp) level and chuck a few letters in such as F, A, R and Q just to demonstrate we are proactive in showing Labour and Green voters how things will be done in this country from now on.
    My officials have informed me that due to the upward testicular mobility (translation: balls up) in certain health sectors, there will be task forces appointed (as opposed to committees) who will be much more efficient – made up of private sector consultants with proven track records in concocting results and efficiencies in these areas (burp). Sixty one objectives is just too high, if we brought that down to just half a dozen, and hence less bureaucracy, we would appear to show the public we are doing something. The resultant attrition of bureaucrats will be offset by them hiring themselves out as private sector consultants on a contractual performance based model (translation: Don't put this in print, but we're gonna turn the whole shit show upside down and put our mates in big bizzo in control and sell the whole fuckin' (burp) lot off to multinational interests, and maybe some time going

forward down the proverbial track when the country's more flush, Labour can buy it back!)"

News: 10 May 2009

"Mr Ryall settles on 3 hospital objectives and 3 preventative health objectives."

"The worst law keepers contend against knowledge. Argue without proof. Hide in bad language, and slow meaningless phrases. Their speech is muttered. They split hairs. They resort to weak unproven statements. Despise precedent. Turn against custom. Change their plea. Incite the mob. Blow their own trumpet. And shout at the top of their voice."

Cormac Mac Art, 12th Century Irish King

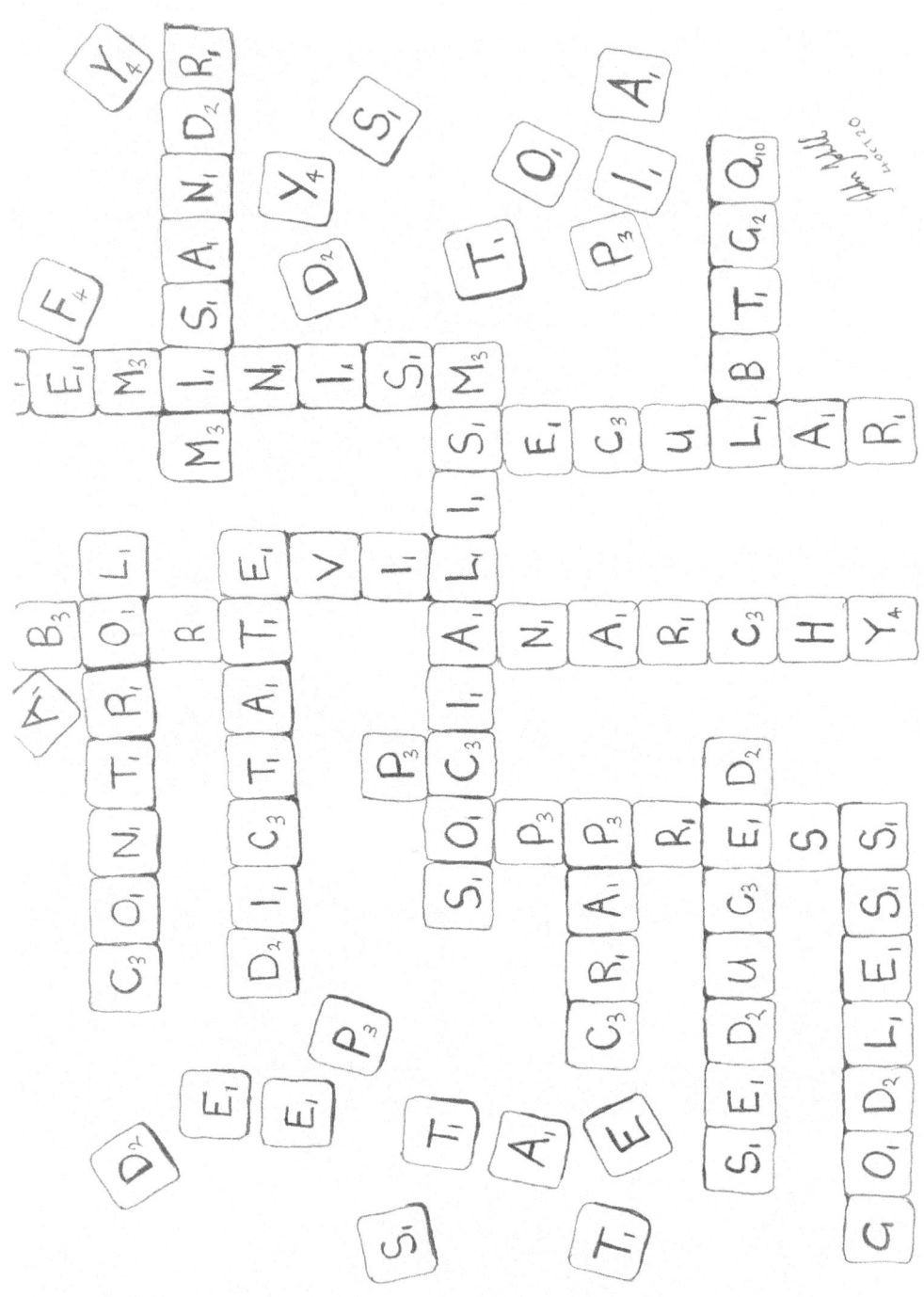

THE EQUATION

Some years ago in the bowels of a prestigious university in a far off distant land – in Europe somewhere but I can't verify that without further investigation by my sources – a bright spark came up with the idea that two plus two equals four.

But......

He exhorted to his students day after day in his lecture theatre that two plus two could equal five: If four hurts a person's (male or female) feelings and causes depression, anxiety and deep seated psychological damage including repressed memory syndrome etc, if a person found four extremely offensive and just another patriarchal tool of domination; or a sexist hierarchical method of making persons conform; If a person wanted to succeed in the futures or share markets; If a person wanted an influential position in the UN; If a person wanted to become a theologian; If a person wanted to fix the world's population problems by entering the reproductive health sector. (This incidentally is booming in Countries like New Zealand, the US and the West including Sweden & Germany) They are trying to export the industry to the Third World, already having great success in second world nations such as Russia and China. There have been no inroads made in countries such as the Vatican as yet, but insiders in the more progressive sectors of the Church in the US believe it's only a matter of time. The progressives in the US church have been into the 2+2=5 theory for years now; If you are a member of the US State Department, Military or the Office of the President. (Successive US presidents have come up with some beaut foreign policy and Military decisions based on advice from experts educated from an early age on the fundamentals of the 2+2=5 theory); If you wanted to become a judge in the European Human Rights Court and to ban crucifixes in all Italian schools. The theory has caught on everywhere; universities, churches, governments and almost every institution, including the New Zealand Rugby Union. Consequently the number of adherents to this theory is not negligible any longer and is increasing every day.

The two plus two equals five theory is simple.

1) Ignore the obvious
2) Ignore history

3) Despise common sense
4) Try to ban the number four in a similar way (using fear) that powers that be are today, trying to ban smoking
5) Achieve this by introducing 2+2=5 theory at early childhood education level then progressively in primary secondary and tertiary levels
6) By putting 2+2=5 adherents in the news media
7) Especially the advertising industry
8) Etc.

From now on, for simplicity of writing and the fact my hand is now getting sore (I'm too dumb to know how to use a PC keyboard so I have to do the old long hand thing) I will call adherents to the 2+2=5 theory, 'Fivers' and the rest of us, I'll call 'Four people.'

The fivers have actually been around from the dawn of history and they seem to have the ascendancy right now here in the twenty first century. It appears, especially to uptight Protestant Fundamentalists and the like, they started in the 1960's in certain respects, for instance during the sexual revolution. But I would say the fivers had a hand in history long before that.

'Somebody' used the theory to convince Eve to pick the fruit of the tree of knowledge of good and evil and also made Adam look the other way. 'Somebody' used the theory to influence Pontius Pilate's decision to let Jesus Christ be crucified. There are a lot of fivers who believe that Sigmund Freud's and Charles Darwin's ideas are great. There were a lot around to agree with Adolf Hitler, Winston Churchill, Mao Tse Tung, Pol Pot, Stalin, Ho Chi Min, Roosevelt, Truman and Idi Amin to name a few. Not forgetting Lyndon, Johnston, Richard Nixon, Margaret Thatcher, the two George Bushes, Barak Obama, and now sleepy Joe.

These are the obvious ones.

A lot of four people have suffered and died because of these fivers. What about your average every day bloke, next door fiver? What about that fiver you work with? If you are a four person these people can make life hell for you too, if you let them. For a start, there is absolutely no way you will convince them that 2+2=4, they will only be offended or insulted. If you're in the pub or at a barby with a fiver and his mates, having a quiet beer and a bit of a yarn is like trying to quietly catch chooks. You will notice they will use the number 4 mixed up with a lot of swear words though. You can only say you are a four person, be an example and hope they will work the equation out for themselves one day.

Speaking of equations, I tried to run with the fiver thing for a number of years, too many as it turned out, even though I came from a four people background. I suppose it came from going to school with and kicking around with the fivers. I think the reason why I eventually went back to being a four person was because I wasn't very good at maths. I had two goes at sitting school cert math; I didn't even try to have a go at University entrance. Physics was the only other option and that left me totally confused, all that mass, energy, time and motion stuff left me cold. Anyway with this limited knowledge of calculus. I tried to apply the 2+2=5 theory.

Things just got more and more complicated. My first mistake was trying to take five away four, this gave me minus one, not a good start, I thought that wasn't right so I multiplied minus one by itself and added Pi root squared and ended going around in circles. I did this for a while and I wasn't happy with the situation so I factored in a couple of integers being sure to punch in a couple of suitable logarithms and what I got was 666.6 recurring, I was not happy with this at all.

This went on for years with numerous variations always arriving at the same answer. Then one day the penny dropped. I remember at the time I had one of those blinding flashes of inspiration. It was an epiphany if you like. It knocked me over, it was simple. I remember I was pretty confused and messed up at the time having been going with the fiver theory for so long. Everything I was doing then was in multiples of five and I was haunted with the fact that my scientific calculator kept coming up with the answer 666.6 recurring. Things just weren't right.

To keep a long story short, I was having a beer with my mate and as usual, it looked like the chooks were going to start flying. It happened when we were on our second beer. Shit, I thought as my mate, who will remain nameless, was cracking open beer number three. There were four empties sitting on the table. Words can't describe how I felt at the time. Two plus two equals four!

The thing is, I didn't need years of education and a scientific calculator to arrive at this startling conclusion. I was rapt. I wanted to share this with my mate but the mood he was in, it would have destroyed him. So I kept this discovery to myself for a long while. You tend to do this being surrounded by fivers. But eventually against all the odds, I became a four person again. I began kicking around with them. Though I still had to live and work with fivers. I noticed there were a lot of ex-fivers who had also chucked scientific calculators away.

NO SECOND PRIZE

But there was still a long way to go before the world reaches the conclusion that two plus two does actually equal four. Here's to the number four.

Postscript

There is one part of the world were this equation is not a problem with the local population. Maybe because their lives a predominance of people of Scots and Irish decent despite religious differences, maybe it's the weather, that part of the world is south of the Waitaki river in the South Island of New Zealand, Otago and Southland to be exact. If you asked the average Yokel down there what two plus two equals, he or she would look at you confused for a minute, then the penny would drop. He or she would give you a definitive answer for that part of the world and he or she would answer – 'about four or five."

THE SLOW EXECUTION

MARYANN THE FLYING FEMINIST

Apologies Monty Python

THE YUPPIE'S PRAYER

Our master, who art in the World Bank
Hallowed be thy fluctuating monetary markets
Thy New World Order come
Thy market forces be done
On the stock exchange, as it is in the commodities market
Give us this day, lots of money
And forgive us our failed ventures
As we send into receivership those who compete against us
Lead us into the Third World for profitable exploitation
And deliver us from the charitable trusts
For the US dollar is the power and the glory
Free market principles forever and ever
For himself every man
Amen

P.S. Please, Father, protect this writer from spontaneous combustion

SHOUT AT THE DEVIL

"Hey you! Yeah you! That's right you!
Let me tell you how it's gonna be
Dirty little worker man
Just like the "New World Order" wants you see
One for you and ninety nine for me
I'm their flunky one two three!
Man they gotta lien on me
That's for sure they own all I have you see
They said "Pay later no worries" to me
How I want to be like you
But pull the plug for sure they would
Should they find out I'd swallowed the pill you take
Oh why me, you dirty little worker man
More than them it's you I hate
Yeah you and you and you".

"Well mister ironmaster rich man
If I may be so bold to say
One for me and nine ninety nine for you
These two coins you spared for me
On your eyes I want to place
It's not my fault you gave your life
To that fool clown Pennywise
Which is to me no great surprise
I was born for to give to you
What's been coming a long time
You've taken our souls and kids long enough
You have the cheek to seek from us
    The justice you deserve".

"We don't really give a damn
What you win or what you steal
With your false precedents and legal ways
We'll never give up while the spirit is here
Establishment is your master and money is your soul
Our job is to make you and hell pay

There are lots of us around
And on the day you'll see who we are
But there's still more coming to the recruiting bus
For every penny you stole we're gonna extract a pound
One day, see ya later Mr Pennywise man."

SEE YA AROUND

For unions struggling all over the world.

HEGEMONY

1. Thanks to the powers that be
   Whoever they are
   Maybe unelected members of our bureaucracy
   Or other institutions like the media
   Thousands of years of common sense
   Have been rendered null and void.

2. Left becoming right
   And right becoming wrong
   Council official Nazis
   Government department and council snoops
   Once they served us
   And now we serve them.

3. Competing ideologies
   Wanting to get into your lounge
   All you want is to watch TV
   At 6 o'clock you hope to hear the truth
   All you get is disasters, terrorists, car crashes
   But you don't get told what is really going on.

4. At the play centre and play ground
   The kids are wrapped in cotton wool
   The swings and slides are low
   Not much of a challenge

Boys aren't allowed to be boys
   And girls paint the boy's nails.

5. The Union movement
   A Labour Party patsy
   The Labour Party
   Self-serving ideologies
   What happened to Micky savage?
   Can academics put food on the table?

6. The National Party
   Political descendants of Massey
   Fat cats reign supreme
   The Ironmasters always get their way
   Our sovereignty under threat
   From their Multi National mates.

7. The Greens demand in Teutonic voice
   Peace, love and tolerance
   Abortions for 14 year olds without parents' knowledge
   And worship of whales and the environment
   Check out the oil burning cars
   With Green Party bumper stickers.

   Where is Jesus in all of this?
   He is with all of His followers
   Who are trying to make sense
   Of the past seven verses
   And yet, He is right there
   In the last seven verses.

Number one
Some people still have common sense
Which is a gift from God
Just check out the Book of Wisdom
Bits of the Koran
And Buddhist writings.

Number two
Some people still know right from wrong
Some are Council officials
Some work for the IRD
Some work hard for us behind the lines
Some are still dedicated to serve us.

Number three
Some journalists wised up long ago
And looked for the Truth in every situation
And not some party line
Or being hooked to some ideology
Or being caught up in prevailing opinion.

Number four
Early education is where you catch a child
Hitler and Goebbels knew that
If you are wrong you have got trouble
For society and the world
Who is educating your child while you work for the Ironmaster?

Number five
Some unionists remember Eureka and the miners
Who fought for the eight hour day
Some "labourites" recognise the value of family life
The foundation of civilisation
And not a society serving a bunch of poofs and weirdos.

Number six
Some Torys are good employers
And reward hard work
Some have a social conscience
But have to toe the Party line
Others champion individual responsibility
But their "Brethren" let them down.

Number seven
Some Greenies are pragmatic conservationists

Knowing that the horse has already bolted
Some have big families
Some actually get off their arses
And do something for the environment
Rather than participate in talk fests.

Some Christians believe in the dignity of all humanity
No matter what their race, colour or creed
They put into practise what Jesus preached
There are Muslims not into beheading
And Buddhists who choose not to kill Muslims
People who put fraternity before bigotry.

Look at the picture of Mother and Child
Does what you espouse or believe in
Or the actions that you take,
Protect that mother and child?
Can that child reach his full potential?
Or does he become another statistic?

COMRADE JACINDA

A DEEP EXCAVATION

The price of smokes has gone up again
Milk, meat, beer and petrol too
Can't make ends meet, there seems no hope
Vehicle import duty has long gone
Car plants have shut country wide
But we are left with smoky hand me downs still.

The population is being disarmed
Goons armed with Glock and Bushmaster
Pepper spray and Tazer for the lucky few
So bury your oily bundle
Under the chook house tonight
In case they come after you.

Dairy farmers and orchardists using cheap foreign labour
Meat works cut to the bone
In the shearing sheds, harder to get a stand
Means more unemployment on the street
Employers don't give a damn
Feed us first – we can't eat your bottom line.

Lots of K Mart and Warehouse crap
A media culture too
In partnership a demand is created
Spoiling the kids, play stations abound
Multinational social media preying on the vulnerable
The bastards have got to be weeded.

Newstalk ZB with Danny Watson
And of course One Network News
Leaving us none the wiser
Just battery fed bullshit
Topics to think about
While we go to McDonalds

Some boys have no role models
Save for the All Blacks
Daughters with no protection
Open to those that deceive
A culture of self-indulgence holds sway
Screaming for rights, but no dues will they pay.

No right or wrong
No black or white
Just grey, no spade is a spade
Tiptoe on eggshells, do not offend
The ogre of political correctness
Is paralysing the truth.

Again, employers demand twelve hours daily work
Extracting pound of flesh, no penal rates
Obscene profits, but for us dirt low pay
Can't afford them smokes
Feel trapped in a rage
It's by the scab we've been betrayed.

The Greens demand Utopia
International conglomerates ignore their children
New Age adherents steal from ancient cultures
The White Anglo Saxon holds the rest in sway
The result, a rejection by the youth of today
The Black Fellas and Indians look in dismay.

How do you navigate all this
Without it getting you down
Turn off the TV for a start
Get the kids off the computer
Take them for a walk
And talk to them.

Get to know your kids
Cut down your working hours

Eat mince and spuds
Play, create and grow
Don't worry about the future
That's easy, you've turned the PC and TV off

Unite, join unions
Claim back the committees and political parties
For the family
Not a bunch of self-serving ideologues
Yeah, brass in pocket
So you can eat steak again

There is help too
But you won't find Him in the media
People want to go shopping
    Even on His day of triumph
They've tried to legislate Him away
But He will have His Day.

PART III
THE PUKEKO LIBERATION FRONT

IMPORTANT INTELLIGENCE GLEANED FROM A GROWING SOUTH ISLAND INDEPENDANCE MOVEMENT.

THE PUKEKOS
WERE GETTING ANXIOUS
AS THE GIANT HARES OF WAITAHUNA

WHO WERE EATING THEIR HABITAT WERE ON ONE SIDE AND A MAN OF INDETERMINATE INTENTIONS LOOKING DOWN THE TELESCOPIC SIGHT OF HIS RIFLE WAS ON THE OTHER SIDE THEY CONSEQUENTLY FELT SOMEWHAT LIMITED IN THEIR OPTIONS SO FLYING AWAY FROM THIS PREDICAMENT SEEMED LIKE THE ONLY RECOURSE THEY HAD OPEN TO THEM. NOTE THE KILLER BEE, HE HAD STRAYED INTO THE PICTURE AT THE TIME OF DRAWING DUE TO THE FACT HE HAD BEEN GETTING INTO THE KOWHAI NECTAR AGAIN AS WAS HIS USUAL HABIT.

THIS CARTOON IS THE RESULT OF DRINKING WHILE IN CHARGE OF A PEN. PERSONS UNDER THE AGE OF 18 SHOULD NOT ATTEMPT TO DO THIS WITHOUT THE SUPERVISION OF A PARENT OR GAURDIAN.

THE POWERPOINT SECESSION SPEECH

As steadfast Southern men straight and true.
I address you at this stage in our history.
Where we are beset by forces from outside.
From up north in particular.
And from other imports who are in league with them.
I am proposing men, that we stage a rebellion.
And that we secede from the North Island.
With their pernicious yoke of slavery.
And all their odd Jaffa ways.
And their seat of oppressive government in Wellington.
Yes we should finally cut the Cook Straight cable.
Which was suggested so many years ago.

We need not look far for our national symbol.
Who cares about the Kiwi and the silver fern?
I propose we adopt the noble Pukeko.
Black and Blue, it's colours we'll fly high!
Because like the Pukeko, it's survivors we are.
We'd expect many refugees from up North.
To join the ranks of true Pukeko's already here.
Queenstown would become a resort for retired shearers.
And Nelson for retired Bushmen and Council Officials.
Unemployment would cease to exist in our new nation.
Anybody needing a job would be sent to the bush.
To hunt and kill the evil Possum.

Many Jaffa – Wellingtonian laws would be repealed.
Michael Laws would never get a visa, even to visit.
The emissions trading scheme would be abolished.
As we know most emissions come from Auckland and Wellington.
There are some from Christchurch and Nelson, granted.
But those emitters will eventually move north.
As we down here generally ignore them anyway.
And as for race relations in the South.
As anybody knows a Pukeko will tolerate anything.

Kaitangata, the Wairua Massacre and Te Raproha notwithstanding.
All Bona-fide refugees would be welcome.

All industrialised dairy farming would cease.
Twizel would be set up as a re-education camp.
For recalcitrant dairy farmers and Fontera staff.
Using the Chinese model they are so enamoured with.
Greenies too, AND the merino would make a comeback.
Rich Italian fashion designers would flock to our land.
Buying all our quality wool and Possum fur.
The Possum would soon become a dwindling National resource.
All visiting trampers to our fair long white cloud.
Would be required to check out at Christchurch Airport.
With at least two dead possums.
And freedom campers would be made to take their rubbish with them

Now here's the sensitive side – ie future investment.
Marriage would be encouraged.
New mothers would receive a five thousand dollar post natal grant.
Funded by the South Island family planning association, SIFFS.
The truth would be taught at schools.
Journalists in our media would be required to report it.
Giving way when turning left would be optional.
The words "A fair suck of the sav" would be in our National Anthem.
All OUR history books would show that Fred Dagg
Was actually born in Waitahuna not Taihape.
We would establish friendly relations with Stewart Island.
And Monteiths and Speights would be brewed down here again.

Kia Ora Kapai and may the road rise up to meet you.

THE BASIC TRAINING ADDRESS (23 Nov 14)
with Brigadier Theodore Churchill

"Pukeko Liberation Front recruits! At ease, gentlemen. I am addressing you at the outset of your basic training cycle which you will find challenging and I'm afraid not all of you will make it, but hopefully some of you will become fully fledged "Good Bloke" members of our growing underground army.

The first combat element of training you will be engaging in is how to subvert the pernicious enemy of our times – and that, men, is political correctness.

As you know, like the Takahae, the average good bloke is under threat of extinction and we have identified that it is, in part, due to our language being subtly changed and used as a totalitarian tool of domination – aimed at subduing Joe Bloggs by certain Educated, mind you, sectors of the Nuevo Post Modern Establishment. They don't like children and think marriage is irrelevant, among other things. This to us is anathema, men!

As our coded PLF press releases state; we encourage "Good Blokeness". It's hard for a man to engage in straight talk these days – you'll just get shot down in flames for stating the obvious. Our adversaries want to shove the truth under the proverbial carpet. We say, no more!

You men, along with recruits from the Women's division of the PLF, will be at the forefront of the battle against these agents of Societal Destruction, masquerading as champions of "equality" and "inclusiveness" – PC terms you are no doubt familiar with.

PC terms will be countered by our straight talking "spade is a spade" ripostes which we will train you to plant at strategic points and explode causing maximum destruction to the house of cards infrastructure of the PC establishment.

Key bastions of this establishment are obviously the Government bureaucracy, for one: district and city councils, the Labour Party and even aspects of the National Party – and, of course, the Greens; Universities; the Feminist Movement; and especially, the mainstream TV news. These are but a few examples and they have one thing in common – the suppression of the Truth. Goebbels would be proud, Stalin would be jealous and Winston Churchill would say "Well done".

You have your work cut out for you men.

Now that we hold the South Island below 45° south, we have the resources and media, namely Radio 4XO, to assist you with your campaign of subverting the unelected powers-that-be and that includes National because half the population did not vote last time.

Note, gentlemen, that Political Correctness is not actually, to use a John Key term, law in the legislative sense but it holds a lot of deluded people under its yoke.

PC attempts to hide the truth or legitimise an untrue or plain wrong activity or action. In fact, one could say that PC adherents engage in linguistic gymnastics and lots of multi syllable words to avoid or pervert a plain truth and replace it with ambiguous language. Without getting too academic I'll hand things over to Dr Dick Shinnery to explain things in simple terms. Over to you, Dr Dick".

"Thank you Brigadier. And yes, you were getting a bit academic there, Brig – the answer is simple men, speak the truth! And use swear words if necessary like 'fuck, you are talking shit you idiot'. They hate it; it leads to them taking Prozac or antidepressants."

At this point, Dr Dick cracked open his first beer. "I'm not gonna beat around the bush men; I'll hit you with PC terms and their PLF equivalents straight away. Here goes.

Partner	someone you shack up with
Termination	the murder of an unborn child
Personal access point	manhole (the imagination runs wild here)
Offensive	well here we go – gis another beer, mate.Ta. Every PC riposte the PLF implements will be offensive to our targets. In fact we are on the offensive. The trouble is, when you call a spade a spade they feel like they have been hit with a spade. GOOD.
Car Enthusiast	boy racer or spoilt little shit who hasn't been taught boundaries by his "progressive" parents and goes on the rampage in his shitty Jap V6, fuelled by Demon energy drinks and Woodstocks. He wears a hoodie while driving thus attracting instant attention from the cops. Maybe I'm jealous – I only had a Valiant AP6 when I was 20.

Bi Polar Disorder	absolute nutter. My mate Sean has Bi Polar and he hates the label – he'd rather be called a manic depressive. He says the label bi polar makes him feel he should be dependent on the sickness benefit but he has a job and can draw and write and would one day like to be as powerful as Winston Churchill who had bi polar too. Besides, manic depression is a good court defence. The life of an MD is a hard row to hoe without do-gooders messing with the label and it's not for trendy, attention seeking fuck ups with borderline personality disorders. Sean's advice to them is to get a life and leave him to shape history along with other great people.
Pro Choice	a spade must be called a spade here, men. It means no choice for the unborn child and soon no choice for the old and infirm.
Mana	proportional to the amount of Government funding a prominent member of the Tangata Whenua has access to.
Consensus	something that happens when not many people are thinking or are too scared to say anything against something due to PC constraints – Labour politicians are a good example of this.
Vertically challenged	short arse carrying the machine gun
Personal Growth	something that happens when you take Prozac, anti-depressants and supplements combined with jogging, using Council provided cycle ways, or hiring a personal trainer, further combined with giving up smoking and drinking beer (but not wine), giving up red meat, taking up yoga, Zumba and or meditation. Not a recommended PLF practice – but we will be there to pick up the pieces. I was talking to my mate, Sean, and he reckons these people could save a lot of money by getting real and getting up earlier, preceded by a good, long sleep.

Self-esteem	up one self. People so far up their own arse they give themselves a bleeding nose.
Self-harm	practiced by young people especially 14 year old girls who have dysfunctional parents who let them spend long hours on social media sites i.e. cliff jumpers.
Dysfunctional	messed-up people who treat their cars better than themselves, They let their "batteries run down", they don't give themselves an "oil change" once in a while, they don't replace their wipers so they can see the road ahead and they let their tyres go flat so the road is hard going. They delight in letting other people's tyres down as well.
Mentally challenged	misunderstood and under estimated people who think differently than the average pleb. They invent things and solve massive equations and stuff but can't hold a banal conversation with their tormentors.
Mentoring	brain washing.
Council Official	unelected, dysfunctional (see previous) official who holds a lot of power over us – need I say more? Sponges off us more than any "sickness beneficiary" or "dole bludger".
Medical Professionals	as opposed to nurses, physios and doctors, they are Herbalists, Reflexology and Reiki Practitioners i.e. quacks – especially Psychiatrists and Psychologists because as soon as you mention Jesus they ask if you hear voices in your head.
Tolerance	what you are supposed to exercise when others are "celebrating permissiveness".
Equal Opportunity	this is where an individual attains a position, not by merit but because they are given that particular position to fill a racial, gender or other quota thus "dumbing down" the position they are given so generously – refer Council Official.

Value Judgement — this little bit of linguistic gymnastics is a cracker! When you point out that a group or individual is doing or saying something that is wrong, they will "scream" that you are making a "value judgement" thereby seriously affecting their self-esteem (see previous).

Gis another, beer. Ta. How the hell is a simple woman or man supposed to navigate all this bloody speak – well, I'll tell you. BY ACTIONS, PEOPLE! By doing what's in front of you guided by right conscience and not worrying about the creepy thought police.

The Irish King, Cormac Mac Art in the 12th century had no time for people who used slow, meaningless phrases and who took a long time to say nothing and who were always on the lookout to correct people in their speech and to set traps – like the old English Court where being politically correct was a matter of survival. We live in a free country, why can't we have freedom of speech? Good people's actions are proved right by history. The perverse PC culture seeks to blot history from the books so our kids can be subjected to untested ideas imposed on them and an unsuspecting society morphed into a civilisation ultimately destined for self-destruction. In the words of J D Blackfoot, "History has named you Savage". The PC culture isn't going to work but a lot of people are going to suffer in the process of us finding that out. Things that are anathema to the PC crowd are honour, truth, honesty, family and good old-fashioned (proved by history) values.

In this PC culture, nobody will be able to think for themselves – the state will do that for them along with the vacuous news media. A public serving the state numbed by social media, the Red Shed, K Mart, McDonalds and an education system championing mediocracy as long as everybody is "safe" and nobody is offended.

The living dead – "1984" George Orwell stuff. The PLF is into life and freedom.

So speak the truth.

Do what is right – not what some academic says is right – and see how it pans out.

And if what you have done is right you might find resistance. But you will be ok.

Thousands of years of trial and error will prevail over the latest intellectual hypothesis developed into a dodgy ideology cooked up by stupid kids prompted by their lecturers who reside in ivory towers and who don't know what the real world is like beyond the university campus. Ironically, most travel a lot but you can't see much of the real world with your head up your arse."

At this point, you may notice that Dr Dick is on a rave possibly fuelled by his excessive consumption of beer, but you have got to realize he works in the academic environment and may have a point.

The Brigadier calms him down. The recruit's attention is riveted on Dr Dick – they are both astounded and impressed.

"Carry on, Dr Dick. Here's another beer."

"Ta, mate. Anyway, back to PC terms.

Progressive	people who believe in abortion on demand: a quick exit for their parents; who believe that somehow less children will advance society. And celebrating the progress of Gay, Lesbian and Transgender people in all parts of society (including Councils, Parliament and Mitre10 advertising). They think this will make our culture great – they don't realize that their ideas die out with them and their self-absorbed children; and immigrants who have a lot of kids will iherit our country.
Flexibility	here's a good right-wing PC euphemism – yes, these pricks are good at it too. It means longer working hours, working "as required", poor working conditions, no smoko breaks, no time and a half, getting rung up by the boss when you are bonking or having dinner.
Bill of Rights	29 ways to excuse you from your responsibilities – enshrined in law.
Respect for others boundaries	this actually means respect MY boundaries and this is just self-focused "me" shit.

Significant Other	now that the words husband, wife, uncle, brother, sister, friend, etc have been superseded, we have this term so the doctor or nurse won't offend anybody when asking who to contact should they need to.
Cultural Safety	this means you are not allowed to offend Wogs, Wops, Kykes, Blacks, Coconuts, Boongs, Rangis, Rag Heads, Poofs, Dykes, Gooks, Spades, Poms, Dagos, Frogs, North Islanders especially Jaffas, Cucumber, Kates, Yanks and especially Canadians – oh and Eskimos if you happen to run into one. We don't have to be nice to Australians because they have a sense of humour.
Key Performance Indicators	this is PC speak for how many fuck ups you or an organisation are making.
Positive Management Meeting	where Key Performance Indicators are discussed.
Inappropriate	language used by resigning employees while attending positive management meetings.
Empowerment	a longing term used by people that have so fucked up their lives that they are looking for a new lifestyle that will give them control over other people again.
Lifestyle	a bit like fashion, really – the latest is "in". It can involve hectares of grapes, a Rockcote mansion and the latest "something" (i.e. gay, enviro-friendly, sustainable, organic) that could get you into the Sunday papers or even on national radio or TV.
Spiritual	definitely nothing to do with Jesus in this context. A Vague feeling of well-being associated with doing nothing occasionally often preceded by vigorous physical activity, sometimes assisted by the ingestion of chemicals or banging on drums at full moon.

Spade	the next word the PC crowd will ban will be "spade". Like manhole is sexist, they will say that "spade" is racist and come up with a title such as "Earth Turning Implement" or "ETI" for short. Imagine all the Bunnings, Mitre10 Mega and hardware stores having to relabel their stock and the subsequent re-education of the gardening public!
Education	more correctly "Re-education" (a Communist favourite) completely turning all common sense on its head and indoctrinating (through the media) an addled, complacent population to be so scared of stating the obvious in order to be completely in control of their minds – Hitler and Goebbels were experts. Ask a young person who Goebbels was and they wouldn't have a clue – I rest my case! A lot of young people hate Jews though.
Gender Reassignment	i.e. boys coming home from the Tiny Tots Progressive Child Care centre wearing nail polish.

The list could go on and on. It all boils down to education, men. My definition of "education" is "free your mind and your arse will follow".

The Oxford Dictionary defines "education" as "bring up; train mentally; provide schooling; train person to do".

Do you want someone like Pol Pot, Germaine Greer, Materia Turei or even Colin Craig controlling you and your children's thinking?

I hope not!

We at the PLF know from experience, as the Brigadier will reassure you, if your mind is imprisoned (by the way you have got the key) you won't go far with us. We are into William Wallace's last dying words before the English ripped his bowels out and that was "FREEDOM".

Do you want it? Will you defend it? Will you die for it?

Will you accept hardship for it? Will you speak the truth?

If so, you might pass your basic training cycle, men. Carry on. Over to you, Brigadier."

"Thank you Dr Dick. Well, men, you are about to embark on a very dangerous period in your training. You will be using "live rounds" right from the start. You will be taught to infiltrate the existing establishment and all that goes with it. You will be on your own with no apparent fire support and you won't know where your allies are. But I can arm you with one devastating weapon of mass destruction and that is the word "NO". Just say it when appropriate and you will be alright.

Remember, men, that the mortal enemy of Political Correctness is good old common sense.

Thank you, men, you are dismissed. Have a feed and then go out there to battle."

TURKEYS

Turkeys and politicians are similar in many ways, particularly in the amount of noise they make when they get together. The difference is, turkeys can be caught, killed and eaten. Politicians are slippery bastards that are hard to catch; they feather their own nests and are generally unpalatable.

Politicians can be like turkeys, but turkeys can't be like politicians.

Rodney Hide is your classic wild turkey – small and scrawny (now) somewhat like a bantam rooster in that he is always trying to prove himself.

Now Winston Churchill, he was another type of turkey altogether – but one Rodney and half the National and Labour parties would like to emulate. Winston(not Winston Peters) was the ultimate politician, in fact Geo-Politician. He wanted to rule the world, but he had stiff competition from Stalin, Roosevelt and Truman, classic turkeys et al. Anyway WC was your typical grain fed, aristocratic, battery farmed, fat turkey and he could gobble like the best of them. He wanted to control the whole barn, as it were. The only time he didn't succeed was against the Turks at Gallipoli, ironically. But like all grain fed turkeys, he died fat, complacent and happy. He didn't see it coming.

Lord Mountbatten was a royal turkey he didn't see it coming either, although some say they saw his tennis shoe flying across the Irish Sea.

Then there was Rob Muldoon, he was called a "Young Turk". Chuck and E and a Y on that and you've probably got the biggest turkey we ever had in the history of Godzone, except maybe Massey, now that's another turkey that nearly ruined the country. He was an Orangman and even today Sinn Fein is calling to have his statue in Ireland, the country of his birth, to be pulled down.

Why is it we always end up with Turkeys running the show?

Normal good blokes seem to turn into turkeys once they get the reins of power. They start wars, rip us off, tax the shit out of us, sell our assets and generally piss us off. We at the Pukeko Liberation Front have decided enough is enough and if we can't beat them we will join them. Armed insurrection is not going to work as the Tama Iti fiasco shows (anyway he is a North Islander and a bit of a turkey as well).

We of the PLF have a new South Island-centric strategy.

We are going to join the National Party and get some of our more respected business and professional "Pukeko" men approached by the Lodge. Then we will subvert both organisations. Secret training will involve our agents being trained in the use of cognac and cigars, flash suits and cuff links. Once this is achieved we will get them working from the inside to right the most evil, heinous and subtle con-job in the history of the South Island. Its making US look like turkeys.

It concerns weights and measures, among other things. Something we as a beer drinking island – excluding Marlborough – have been sucked into. It is with shame I have to expose this. We have been shafted by the worst turkeys of them all – the Liquor Industry.

Our Speights and Monteiths get brewed up north!

But worse than that, it concerns the demise of the swap-a-crate – and the emergence of the perfidious 330ml stubbie. Twenty four stubbies does not equal the same volume as the old 1 Dozen Swap-a-crate but we pay more – we know because we had our Gore University maths experts do an in depth study.

Nobody seems to realize the ramifications of this monumental rip off. Big bizzo Liquor industry turkeys are in the league with the EU turkeys with their standardisation of weights and measures to make it easier to exploit the world and take away our sovereignty.

We pay more for less.

Our infiltrators in the National Party and the Lodge will convert everybody into seasoned beer drinkers, thus they will see the plight of their distress.

We call this "the piddle down theory".

The Liquor industry will eventually be tamed. Alco pops would be banned. The drinking age would be raised back to 20 with anybody underage being supervised by parents only. To cure drunk driving and boy racing a national advertising campaign will run for 5 years and it would ensure that anybody driving a Japanese V6 would be branded as gay.

The half-G and swap-a-crate would be re-introduced. The 330ml stubbie would phase itself out due to another bit of advertising inferring only girls drink out of these. We think this would be an eco-friendly policy saving on mountains of glass. All country pubs would have state-funded courtesy buses.

So far all I've talked about are big turkeys, particularly the Liquor Industry variety. There are more minor, but no less, harmful turkeys, mainly because there are so many of them.

Scratch a greenie and you get a Nazi Turkey.

Scratch a feminist and you get one too.

Scratch a Hippie or a Bogan or a real estate agent, mostly turkeys.

Scratch a New Ager, Evangelical, or "Born again Christian", or a liberal Catholic or Social Credit voter. There are so many, the list could go on and on.

The point is that if any of them manage to impose their nutty views on the rest of us and start making laws then they become Winston Churchills, or worse, Pol Pots. They are potentially dangerous bastards. We at the Pukeko Liberation Front are working on a solution and, unlike Hitler's; it's not a final one.

Ignore the bastards, don't vote for them, give them financial incentives to live in Nelson or Christchurch where we can keep an eye on them. Let them have their own newspapers so that they can read the news they want to read and encourage emigration to the North Island. This we will call our Turkey Minimisation Policy (TMP).

Our research indicates that if the average Joe Bloggs wants to drink beer, eat red meat dripping with delicious fat, be dangerous once in a while, have a WIFE and bring up children without FEAR or favour, these dick-head turkeys need to be phased out.

Turkeys are a drain on the taxpayer.

Shearing in Outback Queensland, Mickey Tohill in yellow singlet

THE PRESSER – OLD SCHOOL

He was born in a cross fire hurricane under a bad moon rising.
He's a voodoo child, a hootchie cootchie man
A man they can't root, shoot or electrocute
He's so hot he plays with fire and never gets burnt
He's so explosive, he's the "H" in "H.E."
He is his Dad's worst fears realised
And damn, his Dad is proud
Because he's another son of a gun.

He can press a bale of wool in minutes flat
Then drag out a few rams for the ganger
And make the best smoko tea this side of the Waitaki
He will take two sweat towels to work
And use both of them.

He'll have the last bale pressed up
And will walk out with the shearers at cut out.
He sews up bales with a spoon needle
So sharp it doubles as a pig sticker.

He can drink beer till three in the morning
And be on deck for the five o'clock start.
You see, to be a presser you have to have heart
Life is short, work hard and play the same
Time for rest when you're dead.

When there's no work he goes to Queensland
No tramp presses and ten dollars a bale
Forty degree heat, Fourex and misfits
Ross River, Q fever and cranks
Skippys abound but you get over it.

He's pressed from Blackall up North
And down to the border
From Quilpie out West and back the other way

Worked with Bill Drury and the Cunnamulla fullas
Out there men are men and sheep are scared.

He's a presser, he's a gun and he will travel
Rousies beware, Cockies lock up your daughters
You've seen Bruce Willis and Arnie on the screen
Now here he is – the real thing
Tell him his bales are under weight, then he gets mean.

He's lean, mean and clean, he's the man
He's the presser
He may be on the run from a past life
He may not just bloody well fit
He certainly doesn't do it for the money
He just does it
He's the presser
His only fear is the Head Rousie
And getting wooled up.

He's the presser and he's good
Only if he makes a good pot of tea
God love the presser
Because nobody else does
Especially if he forgets the tucker box.

CENTRE – POLE

The presser awoke at half past four
He put his mocs on
He went to the kitchen
And joined the gang for a cup of tea
A two hour run ahead.

They went to the wool shed
It was pre-lamb and bloody cold
It was nearly five o'clock
And the head rousie cranked the stereo up
The shearers turned their machines on.

The sheepo was late and he got abused.
The presser having to pen up by himself.
Sheepo arse kicked, the sheep are penned up.
Have a smoke
Suss out the first bale to be pressed.

The AA line is loaded in
He tramps both boxes
And swings the top box over
He pulls the pins
And cranks the handle.

Warmed up, the presser removes the top box
And sews up the bale
In seconds flat with spoon needle.
He pops the box and removes the 195kg bale
Brands out and stacks it, all in minutes flat.

He presses AAA from yesterday
Has a drink of water
And goes to help the useless sheepo
Young prick, just out of school,
Was like that once.

Frog the ganger reminds the sheepo
Of his most important task
To make a decent pot of tea for smoko
And to get some white raddle
For the black sheep he is shearing.

The head rousie is being a bitch
Telling the presser what bale to press next
He knows if he listens to her
He will get woolledup
It's coming on fast.

Too many gun shearers for a six stand
Got to be organised
Stay three steps ahead of her
Go hard
Or go home.

By lunch time the first sweat towel is soaked
Endorphins are pumping
The bales stack up
New Zealand wages
Wishes he was in Queensland.

Back to quarters for lunch
Half bred wether chops
Spuds and really nice salad
The cook from Aussie
She knows how to look after a gang.

Back to work after lunch
Bill Drury is trying to put one around Frog
But Frog stays one up after the hour
Bill will try again, one day someone will
Frog at fortynine knows someone will do it.

Felicity, the uni student
Is getting shit from the head rousie

Who is hard core from Murapara
Felicity starts crying and complains
Head rousie tells her to "handle it man".

The presser likes Felicity
And he helps her out on the board
But Felicity likes Bill Drury
The presser knows his place
One day he'll get lucky.

Afternoon smoko
Some shearers have a grind up
Sheepo fucks up the tea
Frog tells the presser to make it from now on
Presser makes the best tea this side of the Waitaki.

One more hour and three quarter run
Presser slays out some pieces and bellys
And cleans up some of the lines
To make it easy in the morning
Knowing they are going to the Beaumont Pub.

Another nine hour day finishes
Tho five to five really
Presser leaves early for first shower
Cunning is his middle name
All showered, everybody has a three course dinner.

Off to the pub over a winding gravel road
Tim Donnelly's Chev Impala full of shearers
And the Toyota Hiace driven by the presser
Everybody in good spirits
A good days work done.

Some of the rousies stay behind
To go fishing for yabbies in the creek
They plan to have a feed ready for those at the pub
They use bale twine with bits of meat on the end

Heaps are caught ready for the pot.

Meanwhile the rest of the gang arrives at the pub
The Publican smiles widely
Jugs are bought in profusion
Everybody starts talking shit
The Breeze's anecdotes are hilarious.

Sitting around the tables talking inane shit
Are some of the best shearers and shed hands in the world
All elite athletes in their own right
The presser looks on and listens in awe
When the going gets tough the tough get going.

It is now one o'clock in the morning
Frog calls for a round of rums
With an evil grin on his face.
Bill Drury looks lovingly at the uni student
The Breeze and Tim Donnelly want to have a race back.

The Publican calls time with dollar signs in his eyes
He has a special treat for the gang
He passes around nips of Hokanui whiskey
A legend for "Legends"
The boys are well pleased and say good mannered farewells.

The Breeze takes the wheel of the van
Tim driving the Impala
The race back to the shed is on
Thirty K's of gravel road
Two o'clock in the morning.

The Breeze overtakes the Impala
Two K's from the shed
But loses control and goes through a fence
Everybody ok and he drives out the gate
Donnelly wins, only Flemming Noah gets a scratch.

Back at the shed the revellers are met
With a big feed of high country yabbys
They get stuck in and are sated
Everybody talks a bit of remaining shit
And all retire to their swags.

After a short sleep everybody has a cup of tea
And they start another run
Tim Donnelly spews in his fleece
And the shepherds are really pissed off
They have to fix the fence.

The sheepo falls asleep in a bin
Young and stupid – drank too much
He gets shit from Frog at smoko
"You got to handle the jandal"
Frog turns away and smiles to himself.

Horse, the contractor, turns up with some stores
He tells Joanne Kumeroa to enter the Clutha show
She is a good wool handler
One of the best and proud
Not a job but a way of life.

How can a bunch of piss-crook misfits
With buggar all sleep
Manage to do the hardest job in the world?
Though bush men would disagree
Why? Because they have got apple.

Have guns will travel
A bunch of misfit rejects?
Living life to the full
Despised
And bloody proud

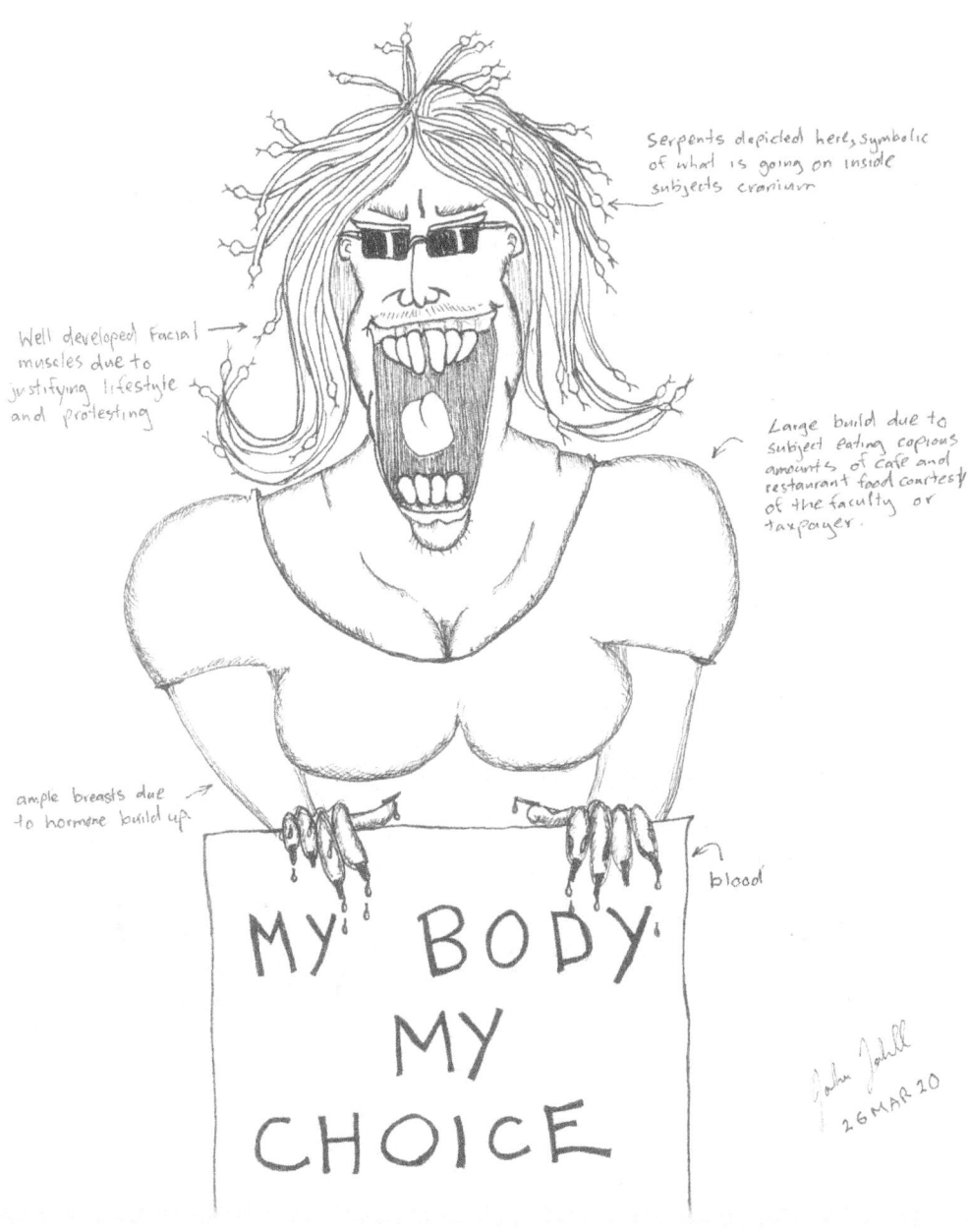

ANOTHER INTERVIEW (DYKES ON BIKES)

"Welcome back to New Zealand, Dr Dick".

"Thank you Sean".

"I hear you caused quite a stir on the Wagga Wagga campus with your lecture on the distinction in meaning between the words 'envy' and 'jealousy'."

"Oh yeah, Sean, I caused quite a stir all right, people are getting a bit mixed up these days with the meaning of words. What with all this P.C., double speak, 1984 Orwellian stuff, it's becoming bloody dangerous these days doing a bit of straight talk. I must say I needed a few refreshments after the lecture. By the way, have you got another beer, Sean?"

"Here you go, Dr Dick. So what was the story?"

"Oh, bloody feminists from some University in Sydney took exception with the connection I made with what they thought was a jealous husband and a jealous God. I thought I was going to get torn to pieces, Sean."

"Shit, Dr Dick! What happened? Here, have another beer."

"Oh Sean, it was hard on the ol' blood pressure. The Femos started shouting, or should I say, screaming me down. They demanded that I quote from their revised, inclusive, no-judgemental dictionary rather than the old Pocket Oxford dictionary that I carry with me. I think the language in the old Pocket Oxford was a bit terse and to the point for them."

"You mean, not open to much broad interpretation?"

"Yeah, that's right, Sean."

"So, what did you do?"

"Well, I stood my ground, after all Wagga was my University at the time."

"You'll have to explain. Here, have another beer."

"You could say I wasn't invited to their drumming in the moon ceremony, Sean."

"Why?"

"I'll repeat what I said so you might get the gist."

"Righto."

"This is some of what I said:

'To cut a long story short, ladies and gentlemen, this is what my Pocket Oxford dictionary has to say about jealousy and envy;

Jealous means watchfully tenacious of one's rights, for example watch with a jealous eye, I am a jealous God, resentful of rivalry in the affection of or on the part of a spouse or rival.

Then it goes on to say; envious of a person or his advantages. This is where I would say jealousy crosses over into envy: jealousy being a healthy thing or even a virtue since God has said He is a jealous God – and envy being a bad thing.' Then there was dead silence, Sean."

"Carry on, Dr Dick. What happened next?"

"I said, any questions before I carry on?"

'YOU'RE SAYING A JEALOUS HUSBAND IS VIRTUOUS, DR SHINNERY?

I think you might have made that connection, Ma'am.

"DON'T CALL ME MA'AM!"

Sorry – Lady.

DON'T CALL ME THAT EITHER!

Any more questions?

WHY CAN'T GOD BE A WOMAN?

I'm not a religious man, it's just what the dictionary says.

YOUR DICTIONARY, YOU MEAN! WE THINK A MALE GOD IS MERELY A PATRIARCHIAL CONSTRUCT PROMOTED BY A MALE DOMINATED INSTITUTION!

I spose you could put a protection order out against Him

DON'T GET SMART WITH ME! YOU MALES ARE JUST NOT GETTING IT ARE YOU? WE ARE GETTING ON OUR HARLEY DAVIDSONS AND GOING BACK TO SYDNEY – SO THERE!

Harley and Davidson were males.

FUCK YOU, YA FASCIST!

Are you travelling over the Sydney Harbour Bridge?

YEAH.

That was built by males.'

"Needless to say, Sean, I got a round of applause. The air of Post Modern Tension dissipated with the departure of the girls from Sydney."

"So, what about envy, Dr Dick? Here, have another beer."

"Good on ya, ol mate, don't mind if I do. The envy part of the lecture was a bit of an anti-climax cos (hic) the ones who needed to learn about it had left in a bloody huff, Sean."

"So what did you say?"

"I just explained what the definition of envy was. The dictionary explains, and might I say any bona fide dictionary should say this; envy is the bitter or longing contemplation of another's better fortune or qualities. I got a bloody standing ovation, Sean. Can you believe it?

You know, I had a thought right then, Sean, and that is along with envy there is a desire to destroy."

"That seems to be the case, Dr Dick."

"And it's in all of us, eh, Sean."

"Yeah, but there's an explanation."

"I think I know where this is leading."

"I'd like to pick up on the God bit you talked about, Dr Dick."

"I thought you might, Sean. Just as long as you keep the Carlsbergs™ coming".

"Yeah, sure mate."

"I'm all ears, Sean."

"Well, you've got to start with the prime mover of the deadly sin of envy, in fact the one who envies the whole human race, particularly women."

"And who is that, Sean?"

"The Devil, mate – Satan."

"Shit, Sean, I thought you were gonna give me an evangelical discourse, not talk about Ol' Hairy Legs. Pass me another beer."

"You know, Dr Dick, if you really want to get to the bottom of what's going on in this fucked up show called the world, you need to identify who's behind it all. Jesus calls him the "prince of this world". A man must get his head around the fact that the devil hates women with a vengeance."

"Why?"

"Because of the Virgin Mary – she gave birth to the One who can save us from being destroyed by Satan. Plain and simple."

"Now you are talking that Catholic stuff."

"Bear with me, Dr Dick. There are two strategies, among many others, that the devil uses to generally cause mayhem amongst the sexes. The first one is where he isolates women from their men in order to wreak havoc in their lives. Women can't do it on their own, they aren't designed that way – either can men, for that matter. The aforementioned feminist movement is just the blind leading the blind."

"That sort of makes sense, Sean, though that view, if mentioned in the media, might be suicidal these days."

"Yeah. The second strategy of Ol' Hairy Legs is to get men, or more correctly, males cos real men shouldn't act like this – to act like complete plonkers thus alienating women and causing them to be isolated and exposed to the enemy's suggestions."

"Some would say that is sexist, Sean."

"I don't give a shit, Dr Dick. That sexist stuff is crap. Men and women aren't equal in that sense. The way some talk, it is that we are two different races or species even, with gays, lesbians, transsexuals and people that like teenage boys all competing for equal rights – it's bullshit.

There is only man and woman – there must be a unity of two. There must be a complementarity of the sexes for society to survive, for the next generation to survive."

"That sounds like common sense to me, Sean".

"It's Catholic teaching."

"So what's the solution?"

"Well, for me as a Catholic it's simple – protect family life. Marriage is the basis for a healthy civil society whether you are religious or not. Marriage was around long before Catholicism."

"So what's the problem?"

"Well, I reckon us men in a general sense have developed a yellow streak. The sexual revolution of the sixties might have brought in contraception and abortion on demand for women, but men brought it about. It boils down to abdication of responsibility and selfishness – the hallmarks of cowardice.

Then there's the males that feminists love to use to stereotype us i.e. men are violent and potential rapists. Geez, I'd hate to be a rough and tumble boy at a feminist child care centre these days, Dr Dick.

They are wrong, barking up the wrong tree, if you like. The problem is with the passive males, the "yes dear" ones. More unborn children have been murdered because of passive males than for any other reason.

Society is in bad shape. Satan works on a woman for the simple reason that she can continue the human race.

So he convinces them men are the enemy – he tries to destroy the 'unity of the two".

"You must find it hard looking around society these days, Sean. Who taught you that stuff?"

"Mum."

"Not the Catholic Church?"

Nah. Mum – and Dad, too".

"So this Catholic stuff is handed down?"

"Yeah, from Mother to son."

"And husband to wife?"

"And wife to husband."

"Gee, that's family alright. How many kids did your parents have?"

"Nine, and we're all dysfunctional too!"

"That doesn't exactly make for a generic Orwellian 1984 world, does it?"

"Nah, you know, Dr Dick, I don't know bugger all about philosophy. Theology, law, politics, science, climate change or population control and I don't really care. But I do know one thing, and this is from experience, and that is that if you have sex outside marriage you are playing Russian roulette with a life of an unborn child and if that child survives the womb, will it have a father, Dr Dick?"

"Let's have another beer, Sean."

"Yeah. Why not?"

"Here's to fathers."

"Here's to the FATHER!"

Note:
This interview took place after Dr Dick Shinnery's one year exchange between Ekatahuna and Wagga Wagga Linguistic facultys.

IN A FLAP - ACADEMIC STYLE

THE FISH

The physics boffins say that a man riding a bicycle is more energy efficient than a condor – which is a big American bird.
Now, just imagine a condor riding a bicycle.
How energy efficient would that be?
Now, stretch your logical imagination here.
A fish is very energy efficient.
The shark is the ultimate.
Imagine the shark, the most efficient member of the fish species, riding a bicycle.

Wouldn't that be theoretically efficient?

Wouldn't it piss Germaine Greer or Gloria Steinem off if, according to logic, in theory a fish really does need a bicycle.

Imagine a fish driving a Ford Mustang
That's a cool fish

Or maybe a fish piloting a 747.
What about a space shuttle?

The trouble is, feminists forgot about physics.

I suppose the logical conclusion to this little bit of theoretical repartee is that fish could actually dominate the planet.

If it wasn't for the Taiwanese and the Russians

THE CIRCLE OF DIVERSITY

"WE DEMAND TO BE INCLUDED IN YOUR SPACE TO MAKE IT MORE DIVERSE AND INCLUSIVE."

"WE DEMAND YOU CHANGE THIS SPACE TO OUR LIKING AND BAN THINGS THAT OFFEND US."

"WE DEMAND YOU BE KICKED OUT OF THIS SPACE WE CREATED SINCE YOU OFFENDED US."

"LOL IF YOU HATE US WHY NOT MAKE YOUR OWN SPACE?"

JEZEBEL SPIRIT?

34th INTAKE BTD

The Southerner picked me up at Milton Train Station, the Bravo Company Pers. From Southland and one from Clinton were already on the train, we carried on north picking up the Alpha Coy Pers. In Dunedin and so on north, basically all the recruits from 4th Otago and Southland Battalion Royal New Zealand Infantry Regiment.

We were on our way to Basic Training. Our number was to be added to by two pers from 3 Auckland Northland Battalion and a number of Armoured Corps pers.

We were to make up 3 platoon, 34 Intake BTD. Looking back, there was a lot of bullshit Bravado and telling jokes on the train, everybody was nervous.

New Zealand Infantry basic training was a challenge even for the Territorials.

We had a lot to look up to, as the Royal New Zealand Infantry Regiment was one of the best in the world.

We knew that, and we didn't want to fuck up.

The public perception at the time was that we were "Cut lunch Commandos".

Not true, we were part time but dedicated.

Most of our senior NCO's, TF or Regular were Vietnam or Malaya Borneo veterans.

We had learnt a lot previous to 'Basic' from then.

Most people don't know, but 40% of the infantry that served in Vietnam were territorial, although they had to go through the same 3 year cycle including one years deployment like all the others.

Contained in my kitbag was a good Iron, plenty of spay starch and a pair of good running shoes.

We were all ready to embark on Infantry training so we would be enabled to defend our Pacifists and Protestors from big Bogies whoever they were.

Our number de-trained at Rolleston Station and were loaded onto RL's (Bedford Trucks) with lots of yelling and abuse.

We were on our way to Burnham Training Depot. On the way overseas my Uncles and Dad had trained there. This place was full of history.

Me and my mates had a lot to look up to.

We dubussed at BTD and immediately were yelled at and abused again.

"Form up in three ranks, you fuckpigs, fucking killer squad alpha, sheep shagging poofters from the arsehole of the country!"

We formed up and digested what had been said.

Maybe we had a wee way to go before these mean arsed bastards accepted us.

Then our platoon sergeant appeared and I thought,

"Oh jeez, who is this guy?"

He was infantry like all of our instructors but had his Beret with the badge in the centre and the beret was turned down on both sides – not regulation.

He also wore this big moustache that didn't look regulation either.

His uniform was immaculate, you could have cut your hands on the creases of his shirt, but he was wearing canvas jungle boots.

What I noticed most was the Special Air Service wings on his shoulder.

Basic was going to be a challenge, alright.

We had formed up.

"Platoon 'Shun, you horrible shower of shit!"

We came to attention and looked at him – a mistake.

"DON'T look at me, I know I look like Magnum PI," he roared.

Someone laughed, he did look like Magnum PI.

"You, you horrible fucking germ. Did I tell you to laugh? Nobody laughs without my pemission. Platoon, give me twenty!"

Twenty press ups. He was as funny as the Gunny sergeant in the movie, "Full Metal Jacket".

As it had turned out, Sergeant "Tip", who I'll call him to protect his innocence, had just completed a 5 year tour of duty with the First Ranger Squadron, New Zealand Special Air Service. We were his first infantry posting since then. He meant business, and we weren't long in realising that he wanted us to be the best Platoon in Alpha Company (coy) BTD (Burnham Training Depot).

We all instantly liked this guy.

Then L. Corporal "Bambi" – who had a reputation as a hard-arse – came into my peripheral vision. (Remember, you always look straight ahead).

I thought, shit, I hope he's not my section 2IC, as it turned out, he wasn't.

Tip screamed in a high pitch, "You will follow Cpl Bambi to your lodgings, the Tai Ping Barracks – Cpl."

Bambi yelled, "Pick up your shit!"

We shouldered our kitbags etc and awaited Bambi's next order.

"By the left, quick march!"

I could see the Tai Ping Barracks 200m away. We were going in the other direction.

"Right wheel."

Some of the guys were struggling with the extra gear.

"Platoon will march at double time, left right, left right, left."

We ran all over Burnham camp, the long way to the Barracks.

We finally arrived and the rest of the NCO's were waiting for us to assign us to our barrack rooms. We were about to eat, sleep, and shit the Royal New Zealand Infantry Regiment.

In my Barrack room, there were two guys from 3 Auckland Northland Battalion, "Roy", "Brad-dick", also "Billy Bunter", "Tilley", "Sid the Cat", "Banana Joe",who was Fijian, a born again Christian from Clinton, and a Red belt in Taekwando from Dunedin.

We were to comprise 2 section.

Back then, a platoon was made up of 3 sections, with an Officer, Commanding PL Sergeant, a radio operator, and "supra enumeres" such as a Forward Artillery Observer, etc.

We met our Room Commander (Section 2IC). His name was "Daz" – to protect his innocence.

He was just back from a T.O.D with 1st Batallion RNZIR in Singapore.

He informed us he was not happy with having to command a bunch of "gay cross-dressing poofters from the arsehole of the country".

We all looked at him with bemused expressions.

"Hurry up and get ya gear squared away, and don't ask stupid fucking questions."

THE MOST IMPORTANT PART OF BASIC TRAINING

The first part of Basic was a shower of shit panic and really hard PT (physical training).

We were issued rifles (ie self loading rifles – SLR's), webbing (Ammo pouches and water bottles with a bum pack worn on a harness complete with field dressing pouch), work denims, packs with sleeping bag ground sheet and Hootchie (tent fly) and also the Yank helmet which I hated wearing, they were called the "Battle Bowlers".

We had to master making up the infamous bedroll, clean the barracks, iron our gears to a high standard, and endure pre-brekky inspection, if you fucked up, you were late for brekky and only got the leftovers.

Tip would always come up with a big ball of fluff during inspections, which decreased as time went by – he used a white glove.

March and drill, march and drill. We were drilled until we became totally sick of it. But suddenly we drilled as one – a team.

Everybody helped eachother out, especially with the ironing – you wouldn't believe how ironing your gears produced team work. We were happening. This was less than a week in.

PT started straight away.

Around 1400 – the hottest part of the day.

You had to get to PT for a start, we had to parade outside the backs in PT kit – shoes, shorts and PTR (a rugby jersey that was reversible).

We double timed (ran) about 2 clicks to the gym. (Very well equipped) and were given tasks. The first early on the piece was the "RFL" (Required fitness Level). This consisted of a 2 mile run to be completed in under 14 minutes as well as prescribed press-ups, sit-ups, and pull-ups.

This was the basic fitness requirement for any soldier. Willie Apiata struggled with his RFL after serving with the SAS in Afghanistan – he had been sitting in Humvees (Dumvees) most of his Tour. The RFL is something that must be maintained all the time.

Willie Apiata can be forgiven, he won the V.C.

CIRCUIT TRAINING

Circuit training consisted of a series of punishing weight training exercises, a one mile run, and this was repeated until the PTI's were satisfied we were buggered, the fitness training instructors were a particular breed of people, some even smoked but man, they were fit. We did cross-country runs (boots optional), sprint jogs, shuttle runs, touch rugby, etc.

We later in Basic realised this was relatively easy. Tip had plans for us.

B BLOCK MESS

Revielle (wakey) was at 0500 and brekky was later in the morning 0700 I think from memory.

In the early stages of basic you had to make up your bedroll and it had to be perfect (a lot of guys struggled with this). Blankets had to be folded x3, with sheets in between with a folded blanket wrapped around this arrangement, it was placed at the head of the bed, with a pillow on top.

These creations were the object of Tip's scrutiny when doing pre-brekky inspection.

Your bed space had to be immaculate with No 1's and work denims ironed creased and starched being arranged perfectly on coat hangers. With boots of course being spit polished. Everything in the drawers of the low-boy had to be folded to RNZIR standard right down to the socks with "happy smiles" and undies rolled up just so.

Many reading this may think this was anal but there is a reason and obviously this has eluded them.

There was a collective punishment if someone fucked up.

This was not getting to brekky on time. The whole barracks including toilets laundry and showers had to be cleaned pre brekky as well.

The stick was the inspection, the carrot was the food at B Block mess.

B Block mess had a reputation for the best food which was famous throughout the Armed Services.

And 3PL always got there first! To brekky that is. Prior to breakfast, we had to parade as a platoon outside the barracks. We were inspected for having a regulation shave, boots had to be spit polished, and you had to have creases on trousers and shirt hence the copious amounts of starch, man we stank of the stuff.

If any dickhead dropped the KFS (knife, fork and spoon) on the way to brekky, we were made to halt and get down for twenty, in fact we got press-ups among other exercises for any minor infraction – it helped with fitness though. But later press-ups wearing webbing and packs were a bit harder.

We would march to the mess and arrive first and this gave us time for a smoke. We filed in. The food was mouth watering, especially when you were shaking off your "civvy" phobias about fat, unhealthy eggs, etc – Bullshit – We were burning off calories at a high rate and man could we eat?

Rashers of the nicest bacon I've tasted, sausages that were real, fried eggs on a bed of white bread, poached eggs spaghetti (Burnham made),

Baked beans, Wheat bix, cornflakes and porridge with raisins in it. Prunes, coffee, tea and milk shakes and also I forgot to mention scrambled eggs.

Being the first platoon in usually we had what we wanted, the last platoon in was usually the Corps Transport (Drivers) they got the leftovers.

AFTER BREKKY – OFF TO WORK

Drill and Marching – it's a very important part of Infantry training.

We bloody marched and marched, 3 ranks, right and left wheel, at ease, attention, left and right turn, salute etc.

With arms, Port arms present arms, attention at ease, Eyes right or left, etc.

It sounds pretty simple – just try it! Most blokes can't tell their left from their right for a start.

If you are marching behind some baggy that is out of step, it's a pain in the arse. In step means working as a team.

Infantry training is about team-work – mates. Like the ANZACS that went before us.

A platoon is as strong as the weakest man. Tip told us that. So if anybody was stuffing up or not keeping up, we were told to help them.

The opposite of civvy life – believe me. Not many of us here were R.T.U'd (returned to unit) from basic. One guy left and I couldn't fathom it, he was a red belt in Taekwondo – maybe he was a hippie. There was another guy – he was a born-again Christian. He took exception to Tip stating emphatically to us on parade that he could walk on water and next to Jesus he was all we had for coming operations.

The born-again chap got through basic but was not happy about the swearing, lewd comments, obscenities, and the general haranguing by Tip and the NCO's.

He learnt to kill the enemy in a basic fashion like us all the same. I saw the humour in it all – maybe because I was a lapsed Catholic at that time.

We had many lectures on all matters pertaining to "minor tactics" (Platoon warfare) and films of actual operations in Vietnam, Malaya and Borneo. We had a demo of the effectiveness of the SLR and M16 rifles.

A leg of beef was hung up in the Butts of the 25m range adjacent to Burnham camp.

The instructor first fired five rounds from his SLR (7.62mm) into the beef. Most of it was destroyed. I felt a morbid fascination with seeing the full metal jacket rounds tearing into the beef.

The instructor then switched weapons and fired 5 rounds from a M16 Assault rifle. 5.56mm. The "16" created 1 ½ inch holes in what was left of the leg of beef. The intention of the instructors was to give us a reality check – it did.

Tip said, "This is what your weapons can do to Nasty Nigel. You are going on the range tomorrow and I don't want any of you to do what you've seen, to me, my NCO's or yourselves. Keep your shit packed tight and do as you are ordered – I can't hear you!"

"Yes Sarge!" we yelled in reply,

I wonder if B Block mess used the beef for mince.

WEST MELTON (THE FIRING RANGE)

West Melton was the firing range during the Commonwealth Games in 1972 I think.

We left Burnham for West Melton in "RL's" carrying a change of WD's (work denims), PT kit, pack, webbing, sleeping bag, liners hootchies, mess tins, etc. And of course rifles, which by now we loved more than our girlfriends. In short, Full Field Service Marching Order FFSMO.

We arrived and got our shit squared away in the huts. The same huts my uncles would have slept in on the way to Monte Cassino and Italy. The same huts Dad would have used when doing his training.

Immediately we got into PT with boots and rifles.

We had a feed at the end of the day and watched a movie every budding soldier should watch – Kellys Heroes.

Daz got his guitar out, then we tucked ourselves in.

We bunked down excited and somewhat apprehensive at the prospect of being on the range the next day.

THE RANGE

The next morning, after breakfast we doubled out to the range with webbing and rifles. We were ordered to quick march once we got close to the range.

Tip commanded us to halt once we got near.

There were some 2/1 Batallion RNZIR guys using one of the ranges. Some were cleaning rifles, while others were shooting. These guys along with the 1st Battalion based in Singapore were regarded at that time by Allied Forces as elite, somewhere equivalent to American Special Forces and were much respected.

We were in awe.

We noticed one guy sitting apart from the rest cleaning his rifle, like he was shunned. Tip explained to us this soldier had accidently shot one of his mates in the ankle on a previous occasion. Simply by not doing as ordered while using live rounds.

Tip said – "keep your fucking weapons pointed down the range at all times. Do you hear me?"

"Yes Sarge!"

"When finished firing always cock hook and look and yell "clear". Whenever picking up a weapon – as we told you to do when you were issued with them, remove your magazine cock three times and point it in a safe direction and squeeze the trigger. This will ensure you and your rifle are safe. Clear as mud fuckwits?"

"Yes Sarge!"

The directive staff had to be anal about this as there was a certain amount of "Buck Fever" going on with a lot of the recruits who had never fired a rifle before.

This was a nervous time for instructors.

This is why you follow orders, this is why you are taught to march as a squad or platoon or battalion.

Imagine trying to train a platoon of radical feminists. The consequences of fucking up are obvious.

Death.

An own goal.

Nobody in the NZ Army has been killed to date in training (as of 1982).

"The object of an Infantryman's training is to give "Nasty Nigel" maximum opportunity to die for his country. Not to shoot each other on the range or during live firing," said Tip.

Later we were to participate in live firing in simulated combat situations with live rounds zipping around metres in front of us.

The screaming and yelling of orders and drills had a purpose – to keep us alive in a combat situation.

Something not self evident in the civilian population as a whole I'm afraid.

There is a reason for rules.

We got into business on the range and to my absolute joy I was getting good groups especially after Daz helped me adjust my sights.

I qualified quickly and I was rapt. Tip said I was a "dead eye Dick". To get a compliment from a SAS man was a boost.

There was only one downside to this though.

I'll explain.

"Billy Bunter" took a long time to get his shooting right, he used more ammunition than anybody in the platoon to qualify.

Cpl Jack called him "Machine Gun Annie".

Billy Bunter would blast away furiously using heaps of rounds until finally when it was his last chance he got good groups.

He later joined 2/1 Battalion and was posted to peace keeping duties on the Sinai amongst other postings. He was probably attracted to the Middle Eastern food – he loved eating.

I remember doing a PT run and I passed Billy Bunter, he was vomiting, he had eaten a packet of chips while we were changing for PT!

Yes, shooting a big assault rifle, a 20 round magazine at a time was cool – exhilarating even.

We were by now getting proficient at cleaning our weapons – and boy, did the directive staff come down on baggys with dirty weapons. We were expected to be able to clean them in the dark.

I remember one recruit who I shall not name saying to an N.C.O "I've got no more oil, Corporal."

Cpl Fred pointed to his front pocket and said "In here, darling."

The guy got his oil but was made to feel a prat – he didn't run out of oil again.

After our time on the firing range and doing PT, we were introduced to basic patrolling, west of West Melton near the Waimakariri River.

We were not issued Machine guns as this was only basic patrolling that all Corps were taught.

Although what we were taught was realistic and very professional based on the Infantry's experience during the Malaya, Borneo and Vietnam campaigns.

Outsiders don't understand in the main that training has a lot more to it than one might think. We weren't just "dumb Grunts" – dumb Grunts don't survive.

"Train hard fight easy"

Training in the Army is a good survival technique right from ironing your shirt to being capable of firing a Carl Gustav anti-tank weapon.

Think about it.

Eyes, ears, reflexes, skills, smarts, endurance, perseverance, heart, bravery, mateship and teamwork to name a few of the requirements a soldier must possess – even a Territorial.

Everybody was getting their shit together a bit by now, ie, had got their webbing (a harness and pistol belt supporting Ammo pouches, water bottles, bum pack and also field dressing pouch and bayonet) fitting right – important. Otherwise your webbing will rub.

We were picking up lots of tips from our instructors. Remember these guys were from 1st Battallion and the SAS – some of the best soldiers in the world.

Don't let some no name loud mouth gym junkie at smoko tell you otherwise.

We felt honour bound to do our best by these abusive bastards. We thought Tip was nuts, but you had to be, to do a 5 year Tour of Duty in the SAS.

The next day we set off with rifle webbing and packs with rations, we wore jungle hats and not helmets. We were heading for the "jungle" training area west of the firing range.

Jungle training area, you say. All you need is trees and scrub. In fact, some New Zealand bush is similar to that in South East Asia, the York Peninsular, or Cairns. It's just colder.

We learnt basic patrolling techniques, the "Triangular Harbour" which is the tactical mainstay of jungle patrol ie; it keeps you alive. We dug shell scraps 6ft x 2ft x 1ft deep; how to use ration packs – a 24hr ration pack can span out for a week.

The unofficial stuff was interesting. Daz was an expert in booby traps and showed me quite a bit, a lot were based on the "snare trigger". Booby traps contravene the Geneva Convention!

When we harboured for the nights, we were told we could be attacked (we were). We were taught how to "bug out" quick. It's an art form and keeps you alive to fight another day. Note: in the Infantry, you don't retreat. You retire or "bug out."

Anyway, we were finally attacked.

I was leaning seated against a tree asleep and it was my turn for 2 hours sleep. Daz was on sentry, I had my rifle on my lap.

We were attacked by the "Enemy Party", they were instructors. They fired blanks and thunder flashes. I was sound asleep and didn't wake up, Daz had to kick me, we bugged out.

Daz later on said, "give me your head". I took my hat off and he punched me in the forehead. A punishment I was to get used to. It was all done in good humour though. You learn to "Commando sleep" when tactical, ie with one eye open.

It was noted by my Instructors that I had a bit of a talent for Infantry tactics.

We lost a Lance Corporal from our platoon. He had been put on a charge for shoving a Corps. Transport. Recruits rifle into his chest for some misdemeanour, I was promoted in the field. I felt honoured, I was now 2 section 2IC (in the field). I was enjoying myself, I was loving it.

I wanted to become a full-time soldier.

There is lots of stuff I could talk about concerning activities thus far – anybody that has done basic training would identify. The rest of you probably watched Rambo, American Sniper, and Platoon, or go to the gym, or do the Coast to Coast.

You can't compare apples to oranges, eh?

GREEN MACHINE

Basic was completed and we dropped the Tankies out of our number, they went on to learn how to drive Armoured Personnel Carriers and to fire 50 Calibre Machine guns. They were later to cart us around Tekapo Training area, in Armoured Personnel Carriers.

We were now into Corps Training.

The Tip informed us in his charming way that he was now going to get us fit. Shit, we thought we were fit.

I have forgotten about our Officers, Louie our Platoon OC (Officer Commanding) a Second Lieutenant and the Coy OC, Major Morrison, a real good guy. So was Louie, he was from 2 Cants RNZIR. Major Morrison was a veteran of Malaya and 1 NZSAS.

"CB" AND CAMP PATROL

Before I get into talking about Corps Training proper, I'd like to talk about two aspects of "Dum Dum School" not many civvys can fathom. I'll talk about the two together because that's how they happened.

CAMP PATROL

Six of us at a time were ordered to the Orderly Room Office after tea in our Number ones.

We were inspected by a Tankie Sergeant, he was a mean bastard who hated grunts, well, he seemed to hate us anyway. He stood in front of me and spotted a tiny speck of burnt starch on my shirt pocket.

"Yer on charge, Fuckpig!" He growled.

Shit, I was going to get "Confined to Barracks", CB.

I was ordered to march the 5 man squad up to the camp patrol hut. There were bunks there, an office and a place to eat. Heaps of coffee and sandwiches.

We were issued with white helmet liners with "CP" painted on them.

Our job was to patrol around Burnham Camp all night in pairs with a check list. We were tasked with making the camp secure, checking locks, etc even though the camp was patrolled by Regimental Police and the M.P's. We did this in shifts, until reveille, next morning.

All I got out of Camp Patrol was missing out on a night's sleep. We were bleary eyed at brekky.

AND I had to go up on a charge!

In the morning, I reported to The Orderly Room and I was "Frog Marched" (ie real fast) by the Orderly NCO in front of Major Morrison. He heard the charge and subsequently sentenced me to 3 days "Confined to Barracks" for this minor infraction.

I was going to find out if I had my shit together in the next 3 days having no spare time.

Being "Confined to Barracks" is not being told to stay in your barracks because you have been naughty. In fact it's quite the opposite. You spend all your down time parading at the orderly room with other "defaulters" doing stupid bloody tasks;

- Push starting an RL truck for a click and then the orderly NCO remembers to turn the key on
- "Change Parades" ie being sent back to barracks to return with an ironed bootlace on a coat hanger wearing number one boots and a PTR wearing a battle bowler.
- CB messes up your gears.
- Report with a lowboy containing certain items (that's a chest of drawers).
- When on "CB" you have to double everywhere.
- Somebody doubling with a lowboy looks funny
- Cleaning ditches
- Polishing lecture room floors
- Sweeping the parade ground
- Anything to mess up your routine

I made sure I never got CB again.

Once basic was over and we were into Corps Training the Tip ramped up the PT, it was really hard, but he made it fun as well. Tip and the NCOs drilled us at every opportunity, and we now enjoyed it.

"Daz" introduced us to "Boogie marching" which the Black American Marines got into – this was always after tea. We had to march (in time) like homies and sing ridiculous shit – it was hilarious and not very Kiwi.

By now 3 Platoon were in Tip's words "becoming switched on proud and alert soldiers". The country needed "Lerts" he intimated.

SHOOTING COMPETITION

A new competition was introduced to BTD and that was a shooting competition between platoons using M16 rifles. The five quickest qualifiers from each platoon from when on the range would make up the teams.

The prize was a trophy with Charles Upham VC and Bars actual Lee Enfield rifle he used in WW2. A mark 2 Lee Enfield.

The shooting competition coincided with Infantry weapons training at West Melton again. Back to the scene of the crime. We didn't know it, but we were in for a big "yippie" along with the Tip's physical training.

Bambi was going on about how all S.A.S training could be done in the Infantry. We were learning that it was obvious. Our sergeant had incorporated a lot of NZSAS methods into our PT, but not only PT everything else as well. We would benefit from this.

Anyway, Tip announced the shooting competition and called out the names of the shooting team. He came up to me and said, "Tohill, you're a useless shower of shit, but you can shoot. Do you reckon you could handle the operation?"

"Yes Sarge," I said. I was rapt.

For the shooting competition, we used Colt M16's "Tonka Toys", "Plastic Fantastics" as we called them. The M16 was the weapon the Yanks used during the majority of the Vietnam war.

With the RNZIR then, Radio ops and officers used them, also lead scouts and medics, etc.

The SLR was still the main weapon used by the New Zealand grunt. It was heavier, but it packed more of a punch. The M16 being only 5.56mm.

The rules of the shooting competition were: Using a 20 round magazine, fire 5 rounds in the prone position at the 300m mark, make safe and sprint to the 200m mark and fire five rounds kneeling on one knee; then run to the 100m mark and fire 10 rounds full auto in the standing position.

Tip said the target by then should be dead. The targets were about 2 foot high and one foot wide and looked rather communist in appearance. Our team got the top score of 95 out of a possible 100.

So there you go, it was a buzz. Tip had taught us a trick when firing prone and that was to bring your right leg up bent on and adjust your aim that way, it works, I still shoot like that today.

Next was weapons training. Each section was issued with a Bren gun and spare barrel and later heavy barrelled SLR's which fired on full auto unlike our SLR's which only fired on selective because of the light barrels which got too hot on full Auto. The H.B SLR's jammed a lot causing I.A's immediate actions.

The Bren is arguably the best light machine gun in the world. Each section (3) had a No1 and No2 gunner, or "gun group". After Basic Training, we used the GPMG and sometimes the old M60 (Vietnam era). The No1 gunner carried the MG and No2 carried his rifle and spare barrel, and magazines for the Bren. With the GPMG, everybody carries as much links of ammo (belts) as they can to ensure they have enough for a fire fight. In fact in a tactical (TAC) situation a grunt is a real packhorse. Thirty five kilogram packs are not unusual for an Infantryman. You "carry your house on your back," as well as ammunition.

As a platoon, it is required that a mortar, aiming stack and ammunition have to be humped. Plus, Claymores Radios, M203's, M72's, + shovels, all on top of gear rations and ammo.

We all had a go with the Bren gun many times. We had a demo and got to fire the M79 grenade launcher, the M72 rocket launcher, Grenades, trip flares. Firing a M72 into an old car was fun but realistic.

Grenade training was strictly supervised by the directive staff. M36 Grenades were deadly and the shrapnel from them when detonated could kill or wound anybody within killing radius.

We also got a demo of a small bag of Ammonium Nitrate and diesel and a plastic precursor and Detonator. This made a big bang and created a big hole.

I thought no wonder the Brits were paranoid about the IRA, they had truckloads of the stuff.

I have often thought that with the thousands of men + women that have gone through TF + RF training and had gone back to their "Valleys and their farms" would be a huge threat to any occupying force in NZ.

What has 700 balls and fucks Nasty Nigel?

Yes, the Claymore Mine. The Claymore is a very effective defensive and offensive weapon. It is particularly effective when setting ambushes.

The Army manual tells you that the Claymore must be deployed a way forward of your position as the back blast can cause problems. The detonation is deafening for a start.

During the Vietnam war, the Vietcong took advantage of this and sneaked up on Yank positions at night and turned the Claymores around facing the hapless Yanks.

The VC would probe attack at dawn and thus cause the Yanks to push their clackers and kill themselves!

Tip's method was to deploy the Claymore in front of a tree or a rock or even a pack. You being huddled behind one of the above when firing the Claymore.

These things fired in a wide arc and killed or wounded anybody in the way. They also stripped foliage off the trees.

Just to change the subject I'd like to mention blisters and footrot which happens if you don't take your boots off regularly, combined with tinia, which you get if you don't wear jandals around the barracks when you're in the shower, etc. We wore jandals in the showers.

This is a problem for Grunts who "beat the feet". The solution is, keep going (don't go on a pussy parade you get behind on your fitness) and use the Army issue foot powder, it works.

Otherwise your "wheels" will resemble plates of rotten stinking meat. I shit you not.

That's not Tip that said that. I'm writing from experience.

BACK TO TRAINING

Our next operation was at Tekapo Training Area. Tekapo resembles Central Otago but without the rocks, it is situated in the Mackenzie Country of the South Island near Lake Tekapo.

Army Training areas are usually in Country that no one else wants.

We travelled there from Burnham in RL's.

Previous to going to Tekapo, we had done a Navigation exercise near Taitapu. We put into practice the use of the prismatic compass and "Lands and survey" maps for navigation.

Resection, Back bearings, etc. The vital thing with map reading and nav, is you need to practice or you forget.

TEKAPO CAMP

At Tekapo we learnt open country warfare at Platoon level. A bridge assault, Chopper Drillswith the Iraqoi: Emplane and Deplane. Armoured Personnel Carrier Drills, Bus and Debuss.

The Tankies that were with us on basic were now driving us around in APC's, they often fired their Browning: 50 calibre machine guns on the drills – yippy!

Better than walking but we mostly "humped it" as the Army was pretty broke at the time.

BRIDGE ASSAULT

We had already learnt minor tactics around Tekapo camp – dry runs in forms of Platoon attacks, defence and ambush, etc. I won't bore you because you've probably watched Band of Brothers Pacific or Platoon. The upshot is really that you keep your mates and yourself alive while killing "Nasty Nigel" and scaring his Generals and Despotic leader with maximum effect.

The bridge assault was a test of our fitness as well as a test of how much we had received in the old "Taringas", the assault required stealth as well to be a successful exercise.

We set off just after dark and followed the road the bridge was on for a short time, then we veered north and traversed a substantial hill, all the time maintaining patrol formation.

We got the brow of the hill and made our way along the north side of the hill so as to not be seen; ie silhouetted.

We crawled over the crest of the hill and made our way down south side to the East of the bridge which was manned by the "enemy party" – instructors.

Tip was with us all the way showing us stuff in whispers. The moon was out so it wasn't hard to be seen by trained eyes who knew how to use their night vision. The biggest thing was to make no noise, we virtually tip toed when we got close to the staging point of the assault.

Our rifles were loaded with blanks and we had BFA's attached (Black firing attachments, which give the weapon recoil so they reload).

We got back to the road this time to the east of the bridge. One attack group was to make their way to an outflanking position to the north on the creek bank, they were to attack first. The rest of us were to attack along the road.

So on Tip's order we attacked.

The whole shit fight lasted about five minutes with blanks and thunder flashes going off everywhere, as the Poms say, it was quite a show.

The "enemy party" on the bridge were satisfied that they had been killed and that their despotic Dictator was getting nervous – "Killer Squad Alpha".

The only criticism was that they thought they saw someone's silhouette on the hill earlier.

We cleared our weapons (a blank can rip your guts out at up to 20 feet), formed up and marched back to Tekapo camp, had a feed and a cup of tea and had a few hours sleep.

SIGN LANGUAGE

How do you communicate if you can't talk or the battle situation you find yourself in is very noisy or if the slightest noise can get you killed.

Yes, you use sign language.

The use of sign language requires team work, mates you can trust and above all being switched on. When voice discipline is required sign language is the only option.

I don't know where the sign language we used came from and it varied from army to army if any at all. On basic we were taught it all the time and we were picking it up.

The Bushmen of Southern Africa are experts and use sign language for hunting where stealth is required. It has been used in the NZ Army for years, particularly in Jungle Warfare operations like the Malayan emergency, Borneo and Vietnam war.

You can use it in a noisy bar. We were taught to use it to save our lives.

NIGHT VISION

Night vision skills were instilled into us right from the start also. It is surprising what can be seen by the naked eye at night, especially in the moonlight. Any hunter will tell you it's essential when moving up to the tops in the pre-dawn gloom. You can see in the dark, you just use a different part of your eye to see.

Peripheral vision is used in the main, you don't look directly at anything and sudden flashes of light destroy your night vision.

Night vision googles weren't widely available then back in the 1980's.

At night if you look at a star or a light in the distance long enough it appears to move and this is a danger for the nervous soldier on stand-to with his finger on the trigger. The apparent movement of lights at night is called "auto climatic illusion".

Using one's night vision is a skill and is essential when technology fails.

We went out to field in full "FSMO" and developed our patrol skills, remember we had a machine gun for each section now and the gun groups got a work out always striving to maintain the higher ground.

Sid the Cat excelled as a machine gunner being only about five foot three in height and of slight build while carrying the heaviest weapon.

Why is it that the short arse carries the machine gun? "Apple" maybe.

As a platoon we patrolled a lot at night. Tekapo is a beautiful place at night, you can't see that many stars or shooting stars anywhere else in New Zealand. There is an observatory at Mount John.

We were introduced to trench warfare. We were required to dig shell scrapes to Tip's standard (1 foot deep, 2 foot wide and 6 foot long). We were always harboured for the night in pairs so two were dug adjacent to each other.

These were connected by a "fire trench" which you can stand in to enable firing from cover. For a long stay in that position the shell scrapes were roofed and the fire trench was revetted (wood and sand bags complete with grenade sump and you might live to fight another day apparently!)

Digging these creations took all night and they were also camouflaged. We were told in no uncertain terms that we would dig faster if we had Artillery pounding us.

When patrolling you dig at least a shell scrape every night when you Harbour. Move, dig, move dig and so on.

We were told the Māori engaged in trench warfare with great success during the Land Wars and a lot of their methods were adopted during World War One.

NOISE AND VOICE DISCIPLINE

One still and frosty night it was demonstrated to us by our directive staff how sound carries at night. Mess tins being used, a zippo lighter being lit and talking could be clearly heard at 300m, scary.

LIVE FIRING

Live firing was not blasting away at targets (not until later anyway), it's the closest thing you can get to real combat it is consequently exhilarating and very dangerous.

We were issued with live rounds of course, each man carrying three twenty round magazines and boxes of ammo in their bum packs. The gun groups had 3 thirty round magazines each for their Brens spare barrels and extra .303 ammunition.

The patrol were ordered to go in a certain direction. The lead scouts were told to look our for targets, the same as the ones on the West Melton firing range. The drill was for the lead scouts to shoot them on contact.

The platoon then went into the outflank drill common to a lot of theatres of battle the NZ Army had been in. I'm not giving anything away in case some gook is reading this! Standard stuff for an Infantryman. Centuries old. We still had heaps of ammo left after destroying the enemy and making his generals panic.

I can safely say that in my time in the army I had fired more rounds – and not only from an assault rifle – than the average "gun nut". Camouflaged baseball caps! Come on, what about breaking your out line? The ducks and deer see you coming!

The best camouflage is faded green or grey or even blue. Black shows up in the moonlight and is therefore not suitable for the average infantryman or woman if they want to stay alive.

After live firing we had a lot of surplus ammunition including M79 ammo.

The M79 grenade launcher is a break open 35mm weapon. It fires a grenade similar to that of a riot gun.

Tip found us a tarn with lots of old ammo boxes strewn about. We all positioned ourselves and were ordered to relieve ourselves of our ammo – yippy!

I had an instructor loading my magazines for me while I was firing at this old ammo box 150m away. I couldn't understand why my rounds were landing short for a start. Then the penny dropped. My helmet was pushing the rear sight of my SLR forward. I rectified the situation and resumed firing.

I fired 300 rounds at that target. The instructor just said "Good shooting bro".

My barrel was so hot I melted an old plastic blank along it.

The Chinese and Russians were getting worried. Tip got me on one of the M79's. I couldn't miss, firing high explosive rounds with these weapons is a buzz.

If you are a Chinese Infantryman in your fire trench terrified that "Killer squad Alpha" is going to attack you and they do firing a 35mm H.E. M79 round from their Grenadaire ie, me into your hole – mate, you are dead.

I suppose my enduring memory from Tekapo was that when you are selecting a sight for digging your fire trench, don't try to dig out an old one as a couple of smartarses from my platoon did. The previous guys had filled it with boulders. I think it was Brad-dick and co.

BACK TO BURNHAM

I forgot to mention the 20 foot wall and the confidence courses.

There were two "con courses" we trained on, one at Burnham camp and the other one "down the road", some miles from Burnham at Rolleston prison.

The con course at Burnham camp had a 20 foot wall.

The object of the exercise to negotiate the 20 foot after completing the confidence course. Remember we were carrying our personal weapons plus webbing. Tackling the wall required teamwork. The wall had no footholds. We used our toggle ropes which we had with our webbing.

This was the only time at basic that were allowed to use our rifle slings. Tip was hot on us not using them – an SAS thing. How can you be ready to fire your weapons with it slung over your shoulder?

Think about it.

Everybody was tasked to get over the wall a section at a time. It took ingenuity and use of the personal toggle ropes, but it happened.

Tip was impressed with us I think. With the exception of Brad-dick and Roy M. we were Southern men pioneers. This was earlier on Basic.

We had managed to evade a hoard of Chinese Regulars. Roy, Brad-dick and our OC were eventually to become members of the 1st Ranger Squadron NZSAS.

Rolleston Prison is a few miles north of Burnham Military Camp. I'm not sure of the exact distance as memory fails me. That was back in 1982, I am writing this in 2018. It seems a long way when you are carrying the Machine gun when it's your turn.

Anyway we doubled there with rifle and webbing a number of times and were told to do the upcoming skill at arms competition on the roads.

After the runs we did the Rolleston Prison's con course, which is reasonably difficult and the inmates would heckle us. But I think a lot of them wished they were doing it too from our side of the fence and running back to camp having a shower and scoffing a 3 course meal, including wicked milkshakes at the B Block mess!

Our next "Operation" was a night ambush exercise at the "Jungle" at West Melton.

You may know of, or have participated in an ambush. One thing that strikes a "newby" and that's that most ambushes are meticulously prepared and once one is set you may have to wait hours or even days without moving a muscle and letting snakes and insects crawl all over you shitting and pissing – self discipline.

I'm not giving away any secrets, suffice to say that the Kiwis had the highest "kill rate" out of all those who served in Vietnam, mainly ambushing the VC.

We were taught by the best.

Anyway Tip told us he was going to infiltrate our position during the ambush exercise at some stage. It was night time with no moon, he said he would shout a dozen of beer to anyone who caught him.

The ambush went off like clockwork and the "Khmer Rouge" were seriously fucked over – none of them survived. Funny that, crossfire is deadly.

There were two os us, me and Tilley who was prone to anxiety attacks, in the rear group ie protecting the killer group from attacks from the rear.

My night vision was intact as Tilley and I didn't see all the flashes etc from the Ambush.

I was peering into the gloom and I saw this flitting figure out to the rear (big mistake Tip). But I forgot the password so I just chucked pinecones at Tip – they could have been grenades. Tilly couldn't see a thing. As far as I was concerned, I had just KIA'd a member of the SAS.

A "REAL PARADE"

The skill at arms was the day after the ambush exercise – bugger all sleep.

What I want to talk about now is the parade before the Sergeant Major of the Army. This guy had risen up through the non-commissioned ranks to become the highest ranking N.C.O of the whole NZ Army. He was much respected and held in awe. He was the soldier's soldier.

We spent hours getting our gears sorted for the parade. We spit polished out boots like glass. Our number one uniforms were creased up to the max. No corps belts yet but we were allowed to wear our berets. This was an honour. How could a civvy relate to this.

The 2nd first battalion soldiers gave a marching demonstration – they made us look a bit average.

The whole of A Coy Btd were formed up in our respective platoons and the Sergeant Major walked along the ranks inspecting us. He passed in front of me and I nearly shat my JG's!

With that over we went back to normal activities.

The whole of Alpha Coy and 2/1 Battalion contingent looked pretty impressive – we had rifles – My uncles in World War 2 had been on the same parade ground too but weren't keen on marching, in fact the Pom's called them "Freybergs Circus". They later acquitted themselves honourably in battle though.

There is not much time for parade ground bullshit when there is a big war on.

They were citizen soldiers just like us a few decades on in 1982.

SKILL AT ARMS

A skill at arms competition is basically a test of an Infantryman's basic skills and readiness for battle.

Our predecessors in the Vietnam era had to pass their Battle efficiency test at Burnham or they would not have been allowed to go. Imagine all your mates going and being left behind.

I am racking my brains at the time of writing as to what were all the tasks we had to perform.

I'll just go from memory.

It was a hot day.

We were broken up into sections, 2 sec, my section had Cpl Fred and 2Lt Louie as commanders. We set off on our run, I still don't know how far we doubled 10km I think.

We were all dressed up with rifles and webbing. Not quite "FFSMO" but that was enough, we had previously forced marched in FFSMO with full packs at Tekapo, that was difficult to do that as an individual. Here we were running as a unit – double time. We all took turns carrying the machine gun.

A few clicks down the road some of the troopies were feeling the weight of their SLR's. We were used to them by now so we resigned ourselves to carrying them at the low port.

Louie halted us.

He ordered us to clear our rifles and attach our magazines to our weapons.

He said to hook our rifles between our magazine pouches and water bottles.

We carried on at the double.

Ah, no wonder he was an officer and later to be a SAS man.

The run was nevertheless a hard one – a test. We finally arrived back at Burnham for the next stage of the skill at arms test.

We were buggered by now.

There were now many tasks to perform, including jumping a three metre ditch, negotiating a six foot wall, throwing practice grenades, loading a magazine in 20 seconds, climbing a rope, crawling under barbed wire, and other tasks.

All tasks under pressure, remember, we had been on an all night ambush the night before.

I tried to catch snatches of sleep, but Cpl Fred kept kicking me awake.

Simulated combat conditions.

We all passed, and I sec of our platoon won the competition.

Tip declared we might be useful riflemen one day.

Some of us were gaining self-confidence, me included, and I don't think any of us thought this was time wasted, including the "Born-Again Christian" dude, because he got the "most improved soldier" award. I wondered if he thought Tip was the nest best thing to Jesus now.

I was rapt and looking forward to "Pass Out" parade and the final piss up.

PASS OUT PARADE

We were doing our gears for Pass Out Parade and were sitting outside with Tip – it was Sunday.

We were spit polishing our boots to RNZIR, no sorry, to Tip standard. Just chewing the fat and laughing with this hilarious, crazy prick from the SAS.

Then, I had a moment, I saw this skinny little SAS trooper march past on the way to the B Block mess, he was about the size of Sid the Cat. He had a maroon beret on, and he really didn't look much like the civvy perception of a giant special forces Rambo Superman.

I looked at Tip and he asked, "Do you want to go to PAP?" (PAP – home of Rennie Lines).

I didn't say anything and carried on looking at my handsome reflection on my boots.

"It's not muscle or brains you need, Tohill, it's spirit or apple",

On the Pass Out Parade, we were ordered to wear our Corps belts. Each Battalion had its own, affiliated to a British Army Regiment. Ours, the 4th Otago and Southland Battalion RNZIR, wore the Black Watch Corps Belt.

A Corps belt is coveted and strived for by the recruit – it means something, like you've earned it.

It was worn with pride.

You don't win one in a Weetbix raffle.

You earn it, along with your beret. Many men before us had sacrificed their lives so some protestor could have the right to free speech. Ironically, the same people who would like to take away our right to free speech!

Soldiers deserve respect, not so ten years after the Vietnam War as was our case. We were ridiculed.

It's not about bullshit British Army tradition; it's about applying a field dressing to your lung-shot mate, and turning him over so he doesn't drown in his own blood while you have enemy rounds zipping aound you and Artillery is exploding everywhere with a nightmare tattoo.

We completed our Pass Out Parade feeling ten feet tall.

Major Morrison inspected us and congratulated us on completing our Basic and Corps training.

The Tip marched us off, and now we only had to hand in our weapons and other gear.

Honestly, I nearly cried when I handed in my SLR at the Armscote, I had become attached to it.

We had a piss up and were Returned To Unit.

Basic is something I'll never forget; it was my rite of passage.

KIA MATE TOA!

LIKE A MUSHROOM

KEPT IN THE DARK AND FED BULLSHIT

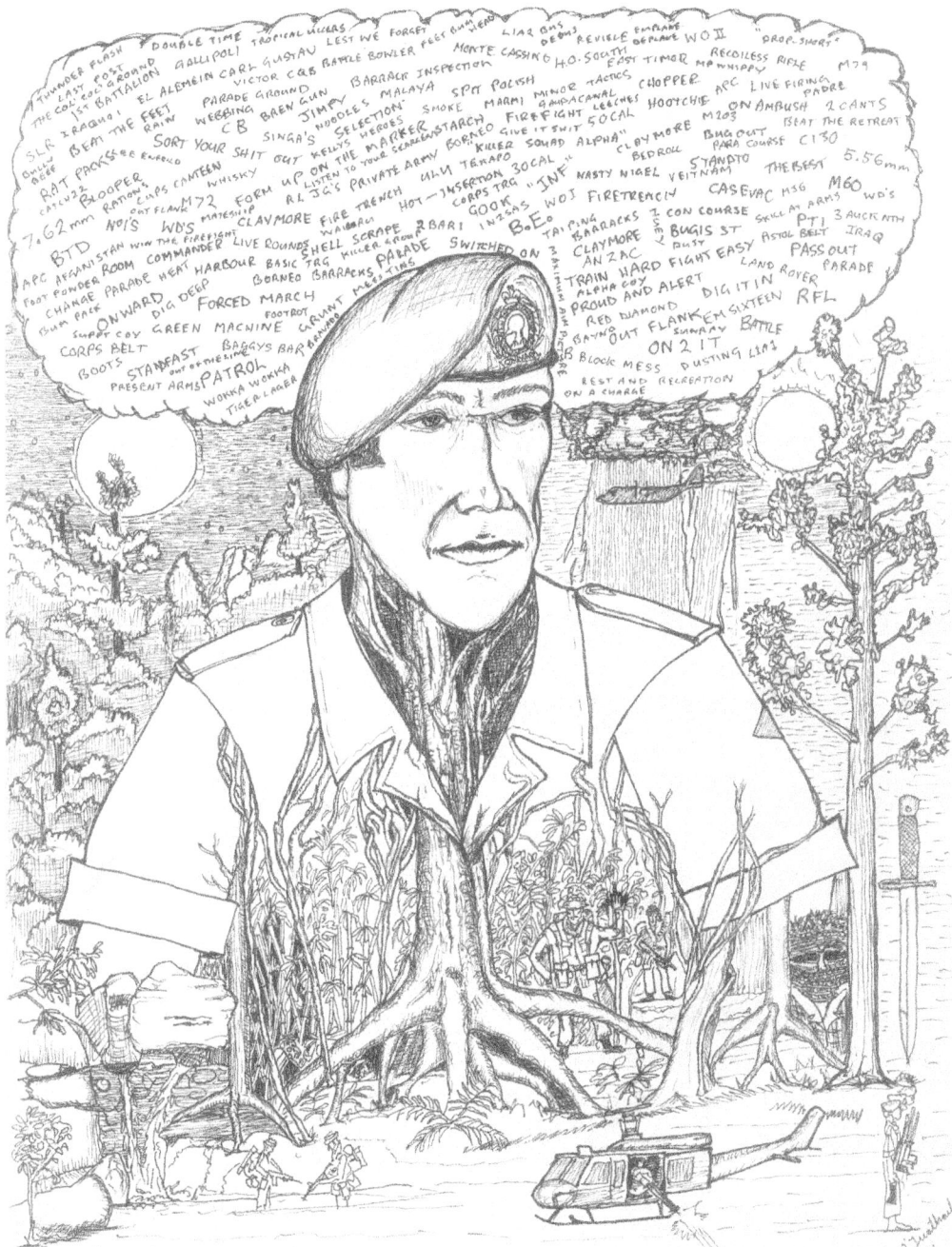

SEVEN POINT SIX TWO

We learnt our left from our right
And what it means to do "stand to"
Six foot by two and one deep
Digging a shell scrape was often our task.

Form up upon the marker
All that parade ground stuff
It instilled teamwork and discipline
Sarge drilled us long after we'd had enough.

Reveille and an early start
The tucker at B block mess the aim
3 PL got being there first down to an art
More time for a smoke after was our goal.

Left right, left right. left right, left,
Double time from the PTI as he barked
Required fitness level must be achieved
We were soldiers from "Four Oh South" – not the rest.

Skill at arms we strived for
B.E. and on the range shooting
S.L.R., M16, Bren, M60 and Jimpy
After live firing time for a yippie.

In the barracks life was hectic
Spit polish boots, iron WD's and number ones
Hospital corners, bed rolls and dusting
Afterwards room Commander produced his guitar.

Sneaky stuff, camouflage and night patrol,
Setting ambush, trip flares and booby traps
Harbour, clearing patrols and sentry,
Just like our predecessors in Vietnam.

Double time with rifle and webbing,
And forced march with pack as well
You think you won't make it
But your mates urge you on.

Getting schooled up on the claymore mine,
What has 700 balls and fucks Nasty Nigel?
The use of the M79 grenade launcher
Fire the blooper and drop it in a hole at 50m.

Live firing the machine gun at Tekapo,
The "Sunray" spots a hare out front
He orders the elimination of the miscreant
The enemy is destroyed in a hail of 7.62.

Our instructors called us "Killer Squad alpha"
A joke but we took it seriously
A real useless shower of shit at first
But switched on, proud and alert for Pass Out Parade.

Achieve your objective and don't give up
Look after your mate before yourself
Hold your head up and look straight ahead
Be a man the guy next to you can trust.

Being part of the best Infantry Regiment in the world
Is something we were extremely proud of
Nobody can take that away from us
Not even this fucked up civvy world.

KIA MATE TOA

SATU DUA TIGA EMPUT
EMPUT RULOH SELATAN

"Instincts take over, you're in survival mode, you're totally, totally focused on the danger or perceived danger either in front of you or around you somewhere. The eyeballs are bulging and you are pumping."

Neville Higgison

If in doubt, cock, hook and look.

"Lao Lao" Tipene.

IF YOU DON'T LIKE THIS "CARTOON" YOU'RE PROBABLY ONE OF THOSE COMMIE PINKO, LIBERAL, PC, INCLUSIVE, WISHY WASHY, DIVERSE, SELF SATISFIED, MARKET LED, SPOILT RICH KID, SELF RIGHTEOUS, OVER EDUCATED, INTELLECTUAL, ARSEHOLES THAT SENT ME IN HERE, SO I'M GONNA JUMP OUT OF THIS HELLHOLE OF PAPER AND PUNCH YA RIGHT ON THE NOSE!

APOLIGIES JOHN CLARK! Seán O'Tuathail 270308

sin-é

WHO CAN REALLY SAVE THE CHILDREN?

"NA ARMA MILISA"
ENCODE, DECODE – ZULU TIME

Let the reader understand:

So people spit at and ridicule you
Everything you are and do
You took up "Queen's shilling"
To escape civil strife and life
Now you are back in their midst
Whether you were blooded on "Tac"
Or a grunt that humped your bread and butter
You retained what they taught and trained
At that oddball school so cool
You gained a degree with honours
And now so very much later
You are still hot to trot
You always feel the urge to boogie
But you can't
Aint that so right
But you know where the Armscote is.

Look at all those big notes about
Jostling you at the bar
In your face
Cut you off in their cars
    You might have one as a boss
Too many silly movies they watch
Not to mention the books
Hoodies and Neanderthal gangsters
Bruce Willis, Stallone, Clooney and Van Damme
Not Black Belts, just Hollywood ham
Mixing up meaning of rifle and gun.

This is what these clowns don't know
With the best we have marched
Never had to borrow real man's blood and sweat

We earned our own
Know Richard Cranium oh so well
Looked him in the eye often enough
Just have to see all and hear all
And tell them nothing that makes sense.

Some of us strived for our "Wings"
Rejected for putting buddies first
Found out later buddies put you last
They were loyal to the
Perfidious Black Watch tartan
The Mother Superior tried to break your back
Along with the RSM and Eagle
Suddenly you remembered your Dad's warning
"Thuggery and buggery they use"
The ANZAC way till they need you
Spit and polish and Number One bullshit
Traipsing around the square
Following someone else's colours
Refused to bite the pillow for him
Redcap howling bastard command.

Stand fast, Kia Kaha, Queen and Country?
You gotta be joking!!
Its hold the dirt for bleeding mates.
My Uncles and their comrades,
    During the two big wars,
Didn't care for that stuff much
At BTD they refused to march
But showed who they were later.
The heights of Casino they did climb
Bayoneting Japs in Singapore
Getting shell shocked in Italy
Hand to hand fighting in New Guinea
Five of my name fell at Gallipoli
Some by Turk machine gun bullet
Some by "friendly" British naval fire.

Look around you now today
Lest we forget the reason for war
Ours is sitting on his Union Jack
He only wants more
With his bloated counterparts
Receiving merchants and traders around the clock
And his lot will till the end
But our day will come.

You and I, what's our heritage?
What colours did our forebears have?
De Bruce and McCartney are tartans
    I have the right to wear
Tara being the primary one
The line I am born to
Also some Norse and Jew
I'm a Mick and a left footer
Fenian my creed
Some would say this is all shit
Some would have us forget history
Burgle our handed down values
And chop us off our line
Do you know yours?
I had to seek out mine.

Where ever we come from
Deep down we know
That something isn't right
We always end up having to fight
Hitting brick walls at every turn
As we open the front door
The back door is always closing
How many times have you had to start again?
Whether you're a Hippie with your plot
Or a sad eyed Kaumatua
A Tradey, a biker, shearer or fisherman
Or any man trying to get ahead.

You have a past, all of you
Some have done hard time
Maybe in the Nuthouse security wing
Or the banging stinking clink
Even worse, a faithless marriage
Dum Dum Skool has kept you alive
You still can't respect the suit'n'ties
Or bosses that promise the sky
Yeah, and the ones that run this fucked up show
They cajole the ignorant plebs
On the other hand they stir up the bro's
Keeping us in covert hate
While they divide and rule.

There is no future in this
We need outside help, reinforcements.
The Kings and Chieftains proud and brave
Of our past couldn't stem the tide
We need a Chieftain acceptable to all
A real man to lead a real man's parade
Also a Brother and a trusted Mate
The alternative is hanging from a rope
Or looking through a peephole
At a turnkey's smirking face
Or being confined with the feral spawn
Of Auntie Prozac and Largactil Man.
Mate, we walk the same road
There's a recruiting bus pulling up
Let's get on board and sign up
And go on the ultimate adventure
Finish your beer and have a smoke
You don't need no gear or money
You will have to be on short notice
For the allotted time and day
You will be told to throw your disguise away
A guerrilla now, but you'll get pay
A Wild Goose armed to the teeth.

This, Mate, is what the Spirit said to me
For years I fought
Not to get chucked on the grate
He told me this when I was worried
That I, for the bus, was too late.
I now see some of the future
He said to me and he says to you
Read very carefully, take a faith leap
And get some ointment for your eyes.

The Spirit said something like this;
"Come to hell with me Troopie
You've had plenty of practice
I will take you back there
Trust in me and you will be safe
Baku Yippie in the dark jungle
You were born for this purpose
Don't worry yourself now
Because you are one of mine.
    You are far out numbered
And hell, excuse the pun,
Nasty Nigel's millions are encamped
In the valley of death and shadow
Listen to them
They bellow like the Hun.

Through that Maggedo I will march you
Ace of Spades we'll deal, by the front I'll lead
Scream and shriek in terror they will
Like their victims ripped off creations wheel
We'll hunt them down to the last one
Throw them into the fiery lake
They'll drown in death and woe

Then we'll encamp at the gates
You will hear the voices of your mates
Shouting battle cries of the past
Those gates won't prevail against our strength

You've kept the Faith despite the weight you've carried
The spirits of long gone ancestors
Who are forgiven their trespasses
Now swell your ranks, give you the strength needed
To carry through the final battle
To free the defenceless
The weak, the meek and the children.

So long, since Adam in fact
They have been in the ancient war maker's grasp
This battle you will win
To make the people free
So they can take their place
At my right hand
Do you know who I am?
Yes, I promise the Kingdom Come
Yes, war is hell and hell is war
But we will finish it, that's for sure
My Father's Grace will see you right
Follow me out of the dark into the light
Take this gun, and with me travel".

In memory of all the men and women who have been killed in the service of the Crown and those who came back only to find that their lives were never the same again.

The Author especially hopes that the reader can grasp the meaning of the word metaphor in the case of this piece.

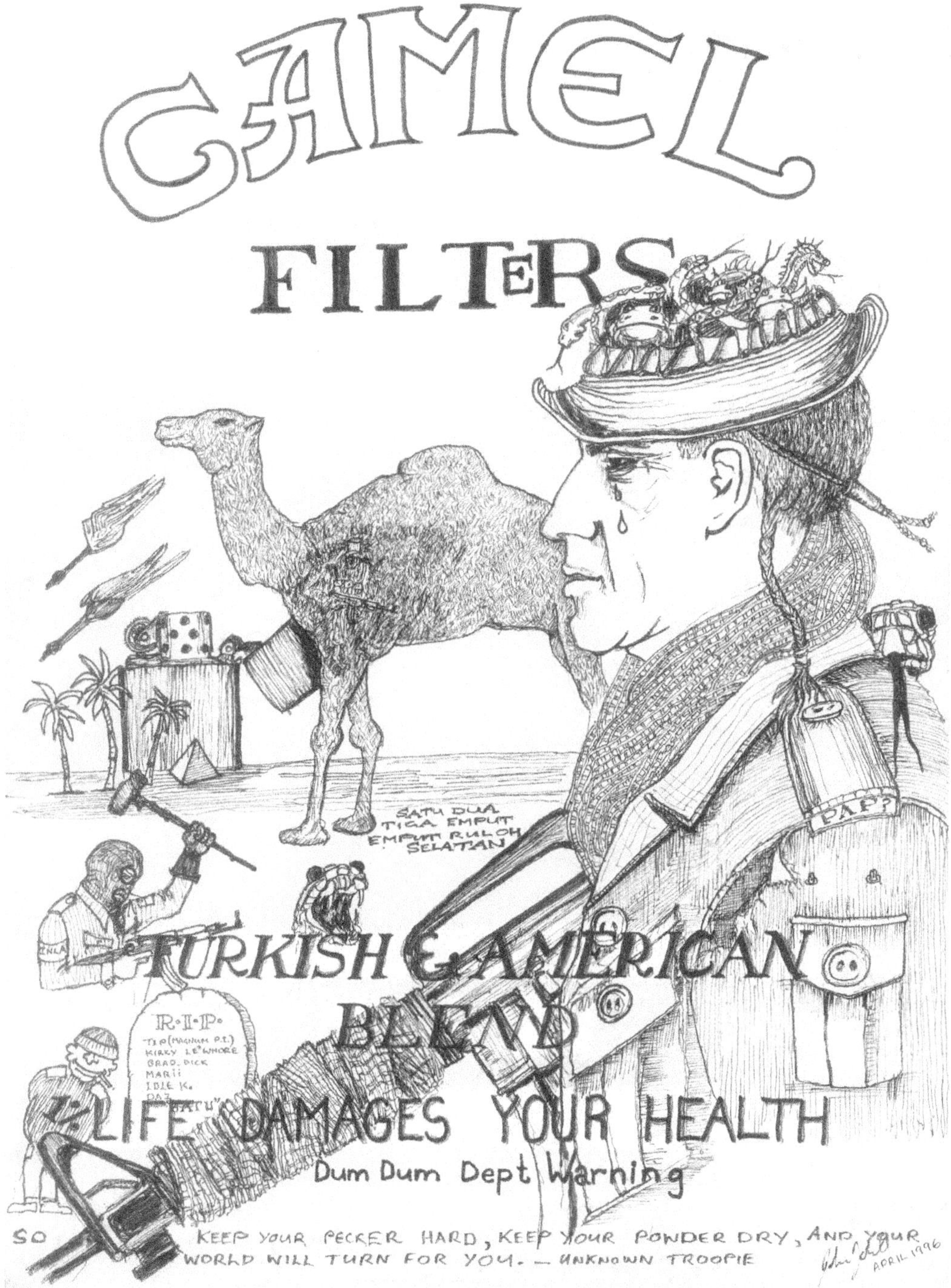

CAMEL
FILTERS
SATU DUA
TIGA EMPUT
EMPUT RULOH
SELATAN
PAP?
TURKISH & AMERICAN
BLEND
R·I·P·
KIRKY LE'WHORE
BRAD. DICK
MARII
IDLE K.
LIFE DAMAGES YOUR HEALTH
Dum Dum Dept Warning
SO KEEP YOUR PECKER HARD, KEEP YOUR POWDER DRY, AND YOUR WORLD WILL TURN FOR YOU. — UNKNOWN TROOPIE
APRIL 1996

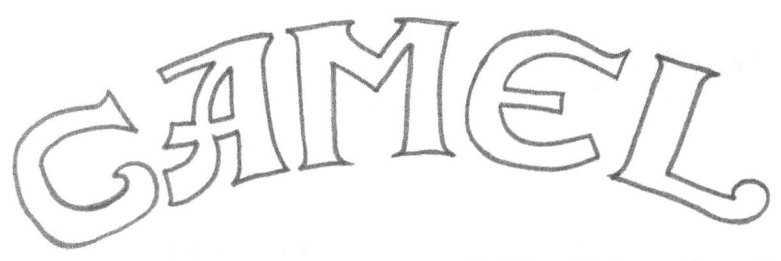

COWBOYS AND INDIANS
(ON PARADE)

Cowboys don't cry
Hear me! Yeah you know
Only Indians cry
You're a hairy arsed bod –
You've ran with the best
You can keep kool
You know what to do
Wait till afta "Skool",
That is the golden rule
You know how to do it
You can "bop till ya drop"
Ya hut won't get burnt down
Cos you know y'aint got one
Hah, you're the Indian
Yeah you know that
You just wear Cowboy clothes
So wait "checkfire", don't cry
Let the "Cowboys" and "Indians"
Do all the shooting
Let the losers ask the reason why.

Yeah you, stand up straight
Don't look at me, cos I know
I look just as I did
That last time you looked
Yeah, a thousand years ago
Look around, three sixty degrees
You know how ta see
Front, back, left, right
Look down at the ground
Where your body will one day be
Look past the sky and SEE
The refuge waiting for you and me
"They" got the lot

But that's nuthin
To what you have got.

Hey, listen to me
You had your arse broken
Many times, you've lost count
But your fires still a stokin
And you never do cry
Cos you're a "Cowboy"
An Indian in Cowboy's clothes
Not this or that or one of those
One of us you are
A man they cannot "shoot"
A man they cannot "root
A man they can't electrocute!

Hey, come on now, don't be shy
Be proud of what you are
So what, you don't have a suit n tie
You won't stand among
Those who have won
Manhood so cheap
By way of a raffle
In the rat race lottery
Check their women out, Blue
Yeah, I'm talkin ta you
How they walk arm in arm
    Her with vasectomised toy
But when he's not lookin
The sway of the hip
The pout of the lip
That secret stare!
Makes you wholly aware
That you got nothing
That he's got
But she wants you
Be a "Cowboy" and don't cry

Cos all she can promise
Is a margarine lie!

So just wait there, troopie
And just hang on
Take a good look
Beauty is only skin deep
Ugly, you may not know,
Goes right to the bone
Let your loins moan
Wait till you get home
Cowboys don't cry as you know
Your crop depends entirely
ON what seeds you sow
And at every "corner shop"
Satan will sell you a bag to go
No deposit, full credit, that's fine
Along with a gooney of "troubled wine"
Buy now, pay later
Just pay the balance at "check out" time

But hey, that aint you
You're a Cowboy through and through
You've taken that bitter pill
The one that makes most spew
Oh me, oh my, you won't cry
Never say why, never say die
Yee ha, live it up
Don't hurt no one
Keep eatin' that humble pie

For "Tip"
Keep cool
Till after school!

THE ODE OF THE UNKNOWN TROOPY

In a firefight there are no heroes
Only the lucky and the not,
The quick and the dead.
If your number is up, it's up
Some men do brave things on adrenaline
A lot of them are unlucky
Some get a medal from the Queen.

Nobody who's been in the heat of battle,
A screaming shower of shit, blood and hot metal,
Is ever quite the same again.
The parade ground doesn't cut it anymore
What's worse, down on Civvy Street,
The reasons for conflict are very evident.

Public opinion will send men off to war
Once again the politicians
Want some more
There are always young men willing to march
That's what the bastards count on.

That's it; the hurry up and wait, the heat and the cold
The dust, the mud, the pouring rain and the leeches
The heavy pack and the long patrols
The stinking rotten work denims, shit rations and no re-supply
The pissing up and the whores.

Years later the long lonely sleepless hours
The sleep walking and chain smoking
And the hard one –
The contempt of the public you served
The two thousand yard stare

All through history men have looked
Down shaft of spear, lance or sword
A Musket, Lee Enfield, SLR or M16

Not at some target or falling plate
No – at some mother's son, brother or mate.

You're told he's only a gook or a raghead
Or the heinous enemy of civilization.
The blood is pumping, you're mates are firing too
You see rounds hit, they might be yours
You tell yourself later they might not have been.
Already done – not much you can do about it
But it stays, stuck in your mind
Mostly down the back somewhere
But it comes up from time to time
Can't drink or drug it away
You just live with it.
You learn to hand it over to God in exchange
For peace of mind – yeah, real peace
Not the peace politicians talk about
The smile of your wife, watching the kids grow up
The Tui and Bellbird, the smell of the bush
The wind in your face, the sunrise
The Land of the Living
Not the Culture of Death.

Jesus' Healing Hand
Only His debrief will do

The Queen can have her shilling back
(with interest)

CRYPTIC UNTITLED PROSE
(7.62 COLD TURKEY?)

Twelve o'clock high, six o'clock low,
No safety catch on and full metal jacket
Collateral damage and maximum kill
Combat elite.

The cold side of hot
The hot side of cold
The darker side of light
The lighter side of dark
The down side of up
The upside of down
The east side of west
The west side of east
Watch out north
As south is coming up.

Then he discovered the up side of fucked
And the inevitable fucked side of up.

Yes, Yin met Yang
Yin made love to Yang
But they never got on
Yang put a protection order on Yin
Cos Yin got pissed,
And smashed a couple of things.
Yang never got over it
But Yin met peace
And they lived happily ever after
Yang got into Eastern Spirituality,
And started a Reiki and Reflexology business.

Dedicated to all those suffering from PTSD

PART VII

"ONE'S TOO MANY AND A THOUSAND'S NOT ENOUGH."
UNKNOWN

ADDICTION

John Jokull
11 DEC 21

TAKE A CHANCE?

"When it comes to taking chances, some people like to play poker or shoot dice; other people prefer to parachute jump, go rhino hunting, or climb ice floes, while still others engage in crime or marriage. But I like to get drunk and drive, like a fool. Name me, if you can, a better feeling than one you get when you're half a bottle of Chivas in the bag with a gram of coke up your nose and a teenage lovely pulling off her tube top in the next seat over while you're going a hundred miles an hour down a suburban side street."

P.J. O'Rourke

I LOOK LIKE THIS TO YOU AFTER YOU'VE HAD SIX OR SEVEN STUBBIES

WORKING HARD

GAME-BOY

YEAH RIGHT – WAYS TO RENEW YOUR FAITH IS SCEPTICISM

When you listen to Jacinda and Joe Biden,
When you listen to John Key and his thought processes
When you watch Robert Schuller and Creflo A Dolar on TV
When you read John Minto's dissertations on things
The fact that Helen Clark has got a top job in the UN
When the Green Party preaches sustainability
When you're told mung beans and tofu will sustain you
When your told abortion is essential for reproductive health
When some Maharishi tells you "don't worry, be happy"
When you observe the reality of the Health & Safety Culture
In fact, when you observe our culture full stop!
When you hear about "Rainbow Youth" teaching in High Schools
When you observe the Café Culture and its adherents.
When the boss starts talking "time and motion and efficiency"
When mountains of recycled and sorted rubbish are sustainable.
When a politician talks about us working longer, harder, smarter
When you go to have a couple of quiet beers.
When someone says we are descended from chimpanzees
(Although sometimes I wonder)
When you listen to "train spotting" Sports Commentators
When you expect the truth when watching the news
ETC………
Is there enough beer in the fridge?

THE JURY

The judicious consumption of alcohol is the general aim of the drinking man. When I say "general", I mean the over usage of the substance aforementioned is governed by certain mitigating factors. And it's because of such mitigating factors said man may use these in his defence concerning the usage of the substance in question. In the vernacular here, with all due respect, he has reasons for said pissed state.

Such mitigating factors are listed below for use where said defendant, i.e. the drinker, is accused of over imbibing by:

- His wife or girlfriend
- His employer
- The Police and judiciary
- Self-righteous church-goers
- The owner of the bar where he got too pissed and smacked some dickhead in the mouth. (Note: the bar owner let the dickhead onto the premises).
- The Alcohol Advisory Council

Defence Counsel raises an objection here at this stage whereby Defendant resents being lumped together with little dweebs who drive Nissan Skylines and drink 6% Woodstocks, and their alcopop drinking girlfriends. Defendant wouldn't be seen dead in a Skyline with some little sninny who won't shut up and actually dyes her hair blonde. Besides, Defendant always deposits his BK and McDonalds litter thoughtfully.

Defendant stands accused by various individuals and groups, here are some other mitigating factors. Further, Defence Counsel would submit that is not alcohol that is the cause of the problems we have in society today but rather, it's over use is merely a symptom of a deeper more fundamental cause.

The Defence would like to respectfully submit that the cause of society's problems is dickheads.

And further that the combination of dickheads and their excessive consumption of alcohol is a bad mix.

Defence Counsel would like to submit respectfully that the judicious drinking man over indulges in the substance on trial only in certain circumstances and under controlled conditions listed herewith:

1. With good mates
2. At Irish Catholic Wakes
3. While NOT driving
4. At summer barbecues
5. After shearing 400 sheep in a 7½ hour day
6. After pressing 40 bales of wool in 8 hours in 40° heat
7. After logging or planting pines all week
8. After any hard work
9. After hunting pigs or deer all day
10. After defending dickheads in court
11. For no reason whatsoever
12. When his child is born
13. The list goes on – this is far from exhaustive.

Defence Counsel would respectfully submit that dickheads aren't capable of doing sub clause 1) through to 10) and in the case of 11) they haven't earned the right to have no reason whatsoever to get pissed, they can only do stupid things for no reason whatsoever – there is a distinction.

And in the case of sub clause 12) their bottle blonde passenger would probably have an abortion and in the case of 13) well, they are only 18 or 19 which negates them from qualifying for the list that goes on because it requires life experience.

And speaking of life experience, working at a supermarket and coming home after stopping off at BK or McDonalds and having a vodka with a demon energy drink chaser and playing Grand Theft Auto or some other stupid game while listening to Marilyn Manson on the headphones, is not life experience – i.e. the list that goes on – especially if they play Warcraft and watch snuffies for rest breaks and go to work or school latently manic.

Defence Counsel would submit that we are raising a generation of dickheads, due to the fact that we don't spend time with our children because we are so far up our respectful (and quite affluent, mind you) baby boomer arses that we don't care any more because we are so busy making money to buy shit we don't need, and saving for our retirement which will never happen because successive governments will keep putting the retirement age up. Our dickhead kids will be too self-absorbed to look after us so it will be left up to underpaid immigrants who don't care.

And what makes it worse, alcohol will be banned, I would respectfully submit that in view of the evidence presented it's no wonder a man imbibes occasionally.

The Defence rest its case.

WHAT WENT WRONG?

"RIP"

Because he's your rock and anchor
You got to love your man
Yes, you must love him
Because if you're cold and hard
Or wily and sweet, full of deceit
Your sentence will sure be given
If not in his life you hold in hand
All ripped smashed and torn
Then maybe at the end of your own
Why do you recoil when you see the result?
When you see him torn and bitten
Slipping, sliding and finally smitten
With the beautiful White Lady
And her attendants cheaper
Whom he knows can take him
To a painless country so fine
Where happiness is in a land
Flowing with rivers of whiskey and wine
He was your rock and pillar
An anchor in a sea of lies
Why do you smash him down?
You build a house out of his rubble
Only for that polluted sea to erode away
Leaving you with a broken island
To be drowned and consumed
In tides of shame and fear
From which he was your shield!
All your man needs is a friend
Evening meals and a warm bed just a bonus
Loving is what he wants so much
Competition and strife have no place
Only leading to his search offshore
In that polluted sea of sex and death
So if he tells of his past and troubles
You be patient and just listen
Don't get on the phone to mother or sister
Maybe he just needs a shoulder

He has trusted you with his dark secrets
Spoken on that pillow after the fact
Otherwise he would've slept with your sister
Or maybe your girlfriend
Telling them all the bullshit
Fathering unknown bastards
Is your man a coward like that?
A clever dick with all the answers?
A dupe with Devil's gun in his right hand?

Well now, forget the past, it's the here and now
As I watch the needle spike my vein
Man! I can't wait for it to end the pain
The money I pay for this heaven
Is nothing to what I offered to her in vain
Body and soul in exchange
For one way sex and soap opera brain

Whoa! Here goes, that hot white blast
here she comes, this is better than sex
A giant butterfly, in my heart and mind
It'll be a hungry dragon later, I don't mind
Shoot me you fuckers, I don't care
No bitch can do this, only my "white lady"
She has no love for sale, only escape
Who cares, the world has stolen mine
In return for Iron Master's rape.

Why suicide slow in those tidy suburbs
Or in dead end slave-like labour
With gutter drugs and gin
At the end of a shot gun barrel
Or with rich and famous lifestyle
Jumping off cliff or hanging tree
No thirty pieces of silver for me
Cos I now take my chance
With the queen o hearts
The joker and Ace o spades

NO SECOND PRIZE

I tried to sort past mistakes
To follow my calling, which is "Seeing"
Through verse and art at the moment
Everyone just covers their ears
They look with sightless eyes
Speak with mouths full of lies
They ignore the smell of shit
That comes from their own blankets
I don't really give a fuck anymore
Maybe this is the last time
I know my sins and I've asked the One
Who created this fine stuff
to forgive all that I have done
Didn't do wrong, I only had fun.

Whoa here it is this time
"Thy Kingdom Come"
"We have come to save you, son
You are just another one"
"Who cares?"
"Well, the Father does, so come".

THE WHITE LADY

She is the instant lover
Who he met in a nightclub
Or on the neon street
Just gotta hand over some notes
His body burns up
He feeds it like a slave
He's got to stoke insatiable fires
Just to feel normal

She is his zippo alight
Urging him to fill his fit
Through that filter and spoon
When there's no money for more
    his baby sends him to the gas station
    Or maybe the chemist direct
With his cut down piece of harm
He thinks that will do it

Sooner or later he'll be crying
Silent tears, being eaten by that dragon
Sitting, waiting and listening
For jangling keys and turning lock
She's in his slot with him
Goading the dragon with his anger
But she is his every desire getting hotter
But his flame burns so very cold

She is his rage, his only protection
Against a world he hates so much
She makes him tough and hard
He knows soon he will be beaten
His arse will be broken
But she will come to his rescue
Selling him cheap wine as consolation
His refuge, he can't let her go

SEAN O'TUATHAIL

She is the promise in the year of Election
And the chapter and verse preacher
The love of control and money
So much like the working girl
Turning tricks by the used car yard
You ask, what chance has he got?
He's got a lot, he just doesn't know it
He can have everything he needs

He doesn't have to go to Satan's store
For a bag on credit anymore
He's sick of tottering down the street
Looking like an idiot
Or nodding off in some dirty public toilet
He's sick of the clink and nuthouse
He doesn't realise it yet
But what he needs is a shot of redemption

He only needs to meet someone
Who will say the right words
In fact, only one or two
Like "no" and "more"
Yeah, no more
Tough love
The arse kicking kind
Pain, the pain of healing

Kicking the White Lady takes guts
A junkie has to dig deep
And find what courage he has left
    To climb out of the deep hole
Before he finds out
Who the White Lady really is
Cos if he does find out who she is
Well, by then it will be too late

DOPE

Roll it up and light
Have a toke and hold it in …. WOW
Let your thoughts wander, too much man!
Did Neill Armstrong really land on the moon?
Toke …. WOW! What if he didn't?
Was it an international Freemason conspiracy?
And, wow man, what about the Twin Towers?
Too much, man!
Toke ….WOW! Turn on the stereo – Pink Floyd, man.
"Two lost souls swimming in a fish bowl, year after year…."
Like, wow man, what lyrics man, they really speak to me.
Have another toke.
Shit, what was that? A thrush flew into the ranch slider window. Wow, far
    out. I hope it's alright man.
Toke …. man, this is good shit.
Turn the TV on
Wow, the Tellytubbies man, far out.
Oh no! Its Tinky Winky, he's scary man.
And that dude inside the sun, totally like freaky.
Another toke….
What's in the mailbox? Go out and have a look.
Far out, that old lady next door is staring at me again – man, her son
    might be a cop.
Usual mail – power, fines, MSD and Baycorp
Stick the mail in the rubbish
Grab the car keys and jump in the Skyline
Dole night – get some BKs and some Woodstocks
Then pick up the boys
Toke …. Oh shit man, it's a bloody tow truck
Backing up the Frikken drive
Bummer man, it's not fair
Watch the Skyline get towed away
Have a toke …. Heinous skunk, man
Go inside, the light won't turn on
It's getting dark
No credit on the mobile

Got the munchies real bad, man
Only cheese, pasta sauce and cat food in the fridge
That'll do, real hungry man!
Mix cat food and pasta sauce together
Grate cheese and fold it into the mixture
Stick it in the microwave
Wow, hunger pangs, need food real bad, man
Like … the microwave is taking a long time to ding
Must be ready by now!
Take dish out, feels cold, consume anyhow
Lick fork and fingers
Fall asleep on the couch
Wake up in the middle of the night with an eerie feeling
Oh no, man, there's a pair of eyes staring at me
From the ranch slider window
Maybe it's that old lady? Oh shit man, freaky!
Jump over back of couch – peer from behind
Oh shit, man, it's only the cat! Oh wow, this is too much!
She's not gonna be very happy with me
Maybe she'll eat the left over cheese
Sleep
There's a knock on the door
Go to the door
Oh no, it's that old lady's son
Skunk is on the coffee table
And he IS a cop
Oh wow, man, life is not fair
The End

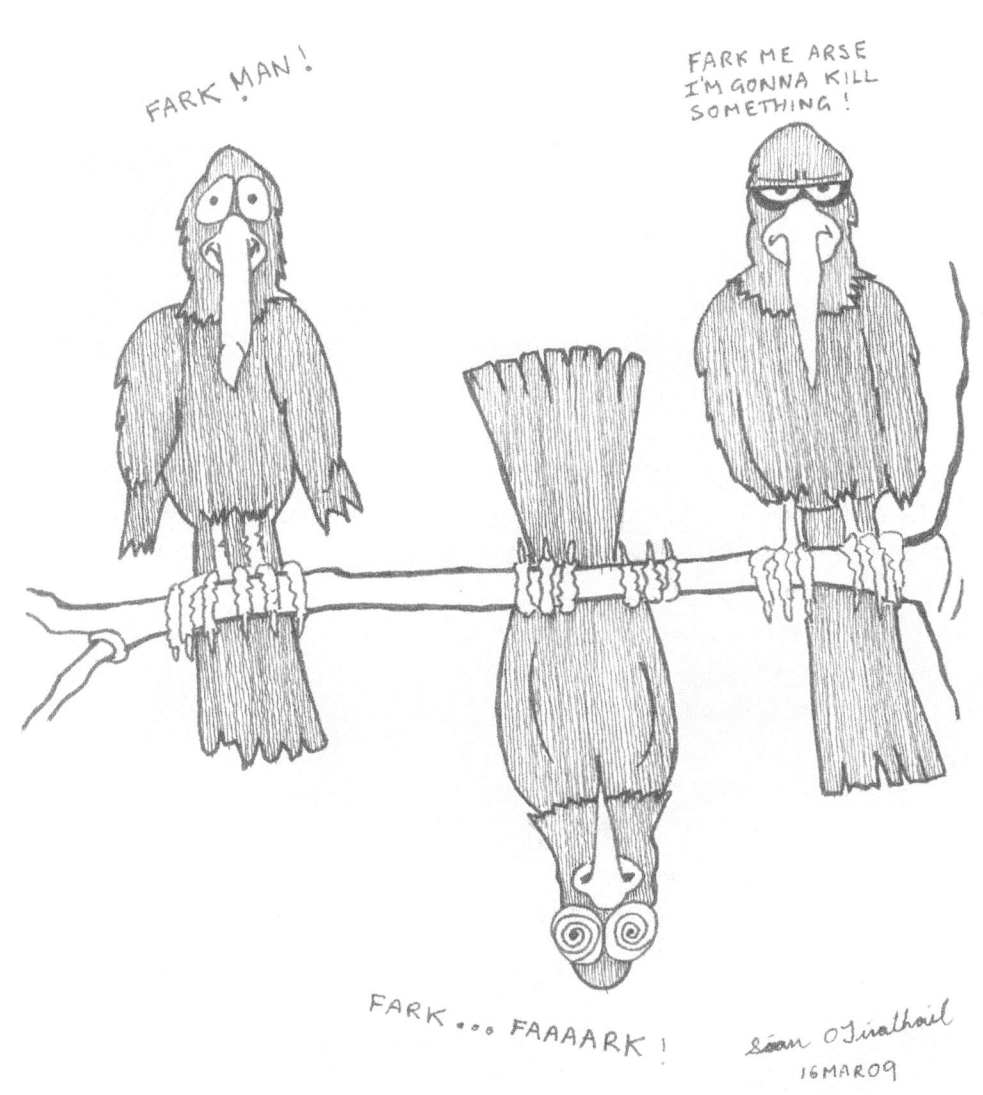

SMOKING AND MISTREATED PORK CHOPS

What a strange society we live in these days where we have "Comedians" leading the charge in the moral crusade department, advising us how to run our lives now that we don't listen to politicians and Church leaders any more. I just heard today on Radio Hauraki the august David McPhail promoting the use of Nicotine patches, gums and lozenges on behalf of Quitline. Without being nasty, but this is the guy who collaborated with John Gadsby on that comedic classic "A Letter to Blanchy". I'm only saying this because I'm bitter – I tried the patches and I'm one of the 50% that fails.

Maybe I failed because I realized, deep down, if I quit I would become like David McPhail?

I was watching the TVNZ "Sunday" programme the other night and who should I see on the screen but that turncoat Mike King, with his sensational secret squirrel, SAS type exposé on how the bloody pork chops I was eating at that present point in time, had been cruelly mistreated.

Those juicy pork chops I was eating, complete with vege and sauce my down trodden wife had submissively prepared, tasted really bloody good, actually Mike. Because I was secure in the knowledge that you aren't funny either and you hold no cred with me, Mike.

I have eaten a lot of wild pork, too, Mike. I ate some in Outback Queensland once, Mike. We caught the little bastard and all we had to stick it with was a blunt steak knife. Piggy screamed a bit. And it tasted really good, Mike.

I know all the P.C., VEDGO, mung bean and tofu eating people who refused to eat meat when they were kids – because their parents where too scared to give them a clip under the ear because they themselves were scared of being rejected as enlightened, progressive parents – will be behind you, Mike. But I am secure in the knowledge that they reside in the trendy suburbs of Auckland and Wellington AND when the power goes off for good, they might have to face reality and go out and get their own meat i.e. kill it, gut it, clean it and try to eat it between bouts of dry retching. In fact, Mike, I think you are such a dick you should advertise prophylactics by sliding one over your head thereby completing the job. Until you find out that whole industry is a con as well.

And what would you do?

Yeah, spill the beans again. You can't be trusted, Mike. I hate you vehemently and I hope you enjoy your very expensive free range pork – that is if you haven't turned into a VEDGO already, and joined the Hare Krishna's.

Signed: Shareholder and member of NZ Pork Board
who will remain anonymous at this stage.
Actually, no sorry, it's just a disgruntled, bored and pissed off
Joe Citizen, heartily sick at the crap the Media dishes up
As news these days. And I'm out in my shed drinking beer
And putting my random thoughts to paper because
My wife won't listen to me any more.
Out here I'm always right.
So fuck the lot of you
I'm gonna have another Tiger lager
With my two best friends; yeah, myself and I.

"HUMAN RIGHTS" FOR THE CLIFF JUMPER AND THE LIBERIAN MILITIA BOY.

PART VIII

MENTAL HEALTH

CASTLES IN THE AIR

Manic depressives build castles in the air
Schizophrenics live in them
Paranoid sentries man the battlements
The Clinically Depressed are chained in the dungeon
Obsessive Compulsives double check the condition
Of the mortar in the walls on a regular basis
Anorexics and Bulimics run the kitchen.

Normal people just cannot get in
Borderline Personalities are not welcome
The drawbridge is raised
When Mental Health Professionals are sighted
Fear pulls the ropes driven by
The prospect of Reality laying siege.

In fact, Reality is the garrison's worst enemy
To the occupants, Reality is an evil entity
He destroys all of their fantasies and delusions
He recommends regular sleep
And adequate nutrition
He has no time for Fear and Anxiety

Reality and his army wait before the drawbridge
He waits because the castle can't last, being fed
By a bunch of Anorexics and Bulimics
And having Obsessive Compulsives scraping away at the mortar
He waits to make his move
Suddenly the castle comes crashing down.

Reality finds a little boy amongst the rubble
A deeply wounded little boy
The boy looks Reality in the eye
He asks Reality; "How can you help me?"
Reality replies, "YOU MUST FIND THE TRUTH
The truth will set you free".

RICHARD CRANIUM'S MID-LIFE CRISIS.

MATTHEW 6:25-34

FEELINGS

Do good – make someone feel good?
Do bad – make someone feel bad?
Tell a joke, say something funny
Make someone laugh?
No, because there's a few things in the mix
That complicate matters entirely.
Apparently there's a right place and time
According to the dictates of this P.C. world.

You can help people – they'll resent it.
You can crack a joke with a cheeky grin.
Many a true word is spoken in jest.
You'll get a reaction like you've committed a sin.
You've done nothing wrong – but you wonder
Maybe they feel bad – a guilty conscience.
You've caused pain – lanced a pussy boil
Hurt somebodies feelings – some sensitive soul
Maybe they needed it – who cares?
Now, wait – the shit will hit the fan
Payback will come sooner or later.

Single issue nutters are good targets
Politically correct prudes are good fun
Religious extremists are a scream.
Feminists – if you like living dangerously
Be careful of Islamic Fundamentalists too
Climate change experts and Greenies.
In fact you can hurt just about anybody's feelings
If you try hard enough
Lesbians, Gays, Canadians, Parking Wardens
Fair game for the dedicated piss taker
People are so funny, they invite satire
If only we didn't take ourselves so seriously
We never used to
Before the advent of Valium and Prozac
What's going wrong?

THE BLUES

John Lee Hooker and Robert Johnson played the blues.
Lynard Skynard and Stevie Ray Vaughn did too.
White or Black, men play blues from the heart.
They've got no message or lesson.
What they sing about is life.
It's ups and downs and what it does to you.
The blues are an experience.
Far removed from depression.
You listen and think "Yeah, I've been there."
The blues don't make you sad, but the opposite.
You realise you're not the only one to be at odds with this shitty fucked up world.
Far from getting down you feel somewhat uplifted!
Because you're not one of those people that gives others the blues.
Except maybe your wife sometimes.
The following is a far from exhaustive list of situations and people that are ingredients for giving you the blues.

- Fat foremen and team leaders
- Some MSD case workers
- Feminists in powerful positions
- Politicians
- Police when they give you a speeding ticket
- Police when they're too busy to catch the guy that burgled your house or assaulted you
- Boy racers
- The TV one news team
- DJ's from Radio Hauraki, The Edge and Classic hits
- TV preachers
- That bloody yapping dog somewhere
- Hippies, vegetarians and conservationists
- Anger management counsellors
- Margaret Sparrow
- The other people that are responsible for the 18,000 abortions per annum in NZ
- The 'Males' that are the cause

- Greedy employers and business men
- People that won't join unions to fight them
- Peaceniks
- Warmongering world leaders
- Sue Bradford and my little sister
- Talk back radio hosts especially Michael Laws and Danny Watson
- People that choose personal gain over the common good
- Priests and Preachers that preach Liberal bullshit
- Priests and Preachers that preach fair right, ultra conservative exclusive bullshit
- Unemployment
- Hangovers
- Cold Turkey and the D'T'S
- Divorce
- Loss of Freedom
- Long working hours
- Bad diet and lack of exercise
- Sleep deprivation
- Betrayal
- When ACC rejects your legitimate claim probably in hindsight because there's not enough money in the kitty due to the fact they've lost money (our money) on (dud) shopping mall investments
- The subversion and perversion of Democracy
- The fact that so many people are wearing high-viz safety vests now that the real workers that need protection aren't safe anymore – think about it.
- The people that drink Demon energy drink and that actually believe there should be 'no laws and no limits'. For every one of them, there are ten who have to clean up the mess caused by their stupid behaviour
- People they call in Queensland 'two pot screamers' Individuals that only need to ingest a small amount of alcohol (not beer because they are too stupid) and then proceed to get loud and obnoxious, smash things up, beat up hapless people on a five to one basis or randomly king hit people who just happen to look at them wondering what planet they've come from
- Oh and while I'm on a rant, those petty officials that delight in telling you, you need a passport or several other forms of identification in

order to complete the form you are filling out, which of course you didn't bring with you
- When you make a simple enquiry to one of the pimply faced snot nosed dweebs at the red shed. The case in point I am referring to was when I asked if the CD 'Double shot of the blues' was available. The young gentleman, at least I think that's what he was, did not have a clue even though the CD had been promoted on the radio for about a week. In hindsight, he probably thought I was some deranged old fart ordering a drink and that I was obviously a bit nuts as this was not a pub.
- The list could go on and on but there is a point where you have to stop thinking and start drinking. Or praying, knitting or something. There is an equally long list of things that make you happy that cancels out the blues.

Life is a bit like the weather really, it comes and goes, there is a season for everything. If you've got a Bible, read Ecclesiastes.

THE LUNA MAN (WIDDERSHINS)

In the waning time,
Of the man in the moon.
The cow had long jumped over,
Gone were the plate, knife and spoon.
He couldn't hear no, "Hey, Diddle, Diddle"
Played by the mad cat with the fiddle.

His dark side consuming did he feel,
Like a mad Banshee screaming,
In his head, dancing some crazy reel.
And like countless times before,
And in cycles to come more,
She started taking over!

Jimi Hendrix also said about it;
"Manic depression
Touches your Soul
You know what you want
    But you just don't know...
How to go about getting it..."

He overdosed and died
Cos' he listened to the pushaman,
Who only ever lied.
Led by the piper so pied
Down the path of false Eden.
    Exchange for that beautiful rush,
Handing over some soul.
For the Devil to stomp into mush!

Yee Ha!
But don't worry, my friends,
Use your talents in the Good name.
Cos' like Jimi and the rest,
Our souls are very strong.
God took the other ninety nine percent.

A COMPOSITE ANECDOTE

(Read this really fast)

He woke up. It was 0330
He felt good
In fact, he felt really good lately
He'd stopped taking his medication 2 weeks ago
Because he felt so bloody good
He didn't need this shit anymore
Fucking Shrinks!

He did a couple of back flips and a hundred press-ups
Then he made a strong perk coffee
It was now 0430
Shop must be open. Need some Red Bulls
Go to 24hour petrol station instead
Buy a dozen Red Bulls.

Have an in-depth conversation
With the guy at counter
About Vladimir Putin's expansionist plans in Ukraine
Guy at counter seems agitated
He points out the growing queue
Titchy little bastard, he thinks.
He tells him to cool it and leaves
Some people!

Get back into the old SUV
Oil light on – never mind
Let's go for a drive, take a detour home
100kmh around the side streets
Yippy! It's now 0530
Whoa, what a noise coming from the engine
Grind to a halt.

Where am I? Got work at seven
Start walking – take the Red Bulls

Arrive at building site late
Left tools in the old SUV
Unable to lock it
Tell Boss the story.
After 30 minutes, boss replies
"You are sacked, you idiot"
Boss obviously didn't like the perfectly reasonable story
Of trying to explain the Ukrainian situation
To the titchy servo attendant
And how he made him forget to put oil in the engine.

"Fuck your job, anyway,
You fuckin arsehole.
I'm gonna start out on my own
And put you out of fuckin business
You prick!"
Boss laughs

Our man heads for home
Only two Red Bulls left
He stops at liquor store
Buys a 40oz Vodka and more Red Bulls
Walks down the street swinging from the lampposts
Sings "I believe I could fly"

Suddenly he spots a record store
He goes in.
He engages the proprietor in a discussion
On the existence of Angels
The proprietor smiles and points him to L for Led Zeppelin
Our man buys the whole collection.

Armed with the entire Led Zeppelin collection,
The Vodka and the Red Bulls
He carries on home.
On the way he decides he is a shaman
Only a shaman could think like he does
He will tell his neighbour,
The pretty girl next door.

He spots a car sales yard
Look at that, an '85 BMW!
He engages the car salesman
In a one way conversation
Concerning Saddam Hussein
Fifth century Irish monks
And modern day shamans, of which he is one,
And also the fall of the Incas.

Ever hopeful, the car salesman listens
While getting the papers to sign
Our man promises to pay the balance
When his building firm is up and running
He uses his eftpos card for the deposit
Amazingly, it accepts!

The car salesman smiles
Now all our man has to do
Is pay $250 per week for 36 months
Easy – he'll be rich anyway
Drives home in newly acquired BMW
Arrives.....
He puts Led Zeppelin 1 on his stereo
And turns up the volume
Makes up a vodka Red Bull
Maybe Cindy next door would like one?
He goes over
Cindy is wearing a low cut slip. Wow!

She lets him in.
They have some VRB's and smoke some weed
He tells her he is a shaman
She believes him
They have amazing sex
She is hooked.

"Let's go for a drive in my new car!"
They go for a drive

100kmh around side streets
    More sex in the back seat
Back home.

Led Zeppelin 2, 3 and 4
At full volume
More VRB's, dope and amazing sex
Or so he thought
It is now 2300
"Let's go night clubbing!" he said.

Cindy agreed on one condition
That they take a taxi
Off they go
He has an amazing conversation
With the Iraqi taxi driver
Saddam, ISIS, the Tower of Babel and Burkhas
He thought they were instant friends
The Iraqi taxi driver stops short of their destination
And demands they pay their fare and get out

He wonders why everybody
Is being so agro today
They walk the rest of the way
Cindy breaks the heel of her shoe
He convinces her to go barefoot
As it looks so cool. She does.

They get to the night club door
He has an in-depth conversation with the Doormen
Things don't go so well
They refuse him entry
He shouts over his shoulder that they are puppets
With Satan's hand up their arses.

This amuses the Doormen
He shouts that he is a shaman
Well practised in third eye techniques

This the Doormen also find amusing
He turns round to find Cindy getting into a taxi
He chases after it to no avail.

He comes across an alley
He enters and finds a group of Hoodies there
He has an amazing conversation with them
They promptly beat the shit out of them
He is taken to Casualty by the Cops
He has an amazing conversation with the staff at the hospital
They discharge him after patching him up.

He gets a taxi home and picks up some Woodstocks on the way
He gets home and puts Physical Graffiti on
Full volume
It's now 0730
He knocks on Cindy's door
She answers. She is crying
She says it's over and she's tired
Embarrassed and pissed off
He doesn't understand
He puts on Led Zeppelin 1 again
And ploughs through the Woodstocks
He decides to play "You Shook Me" on repeat
He finds some paint and paints his face
Like a Cherokee shaman / medicine man

He goes to the bathroom and looks in the mirror
He shaves his head
Like a 5th century Irish monk
And dances to "You Shook Me"
Full volume
He believes he can fly.

So he climbs up on the roof
He can see angels hovering over the city
He calls to them
He sees some bikers riding past

He thinks they are angels from hell
He screams for God to help him
No answer

He sees a police car coming up the drive
The cops ask what he is doing up there
He says he is a shamanic SAS trooper
Practising his final jump
The cops persuade him to come down
Finally.

They ask him about his haircut
He says he is descended
From a 5th century Irish monk
"Really", they say with a smile
Finally he is taken to the cells
While the cops call the Mental Health Crisis Team

He doesn't like the cell
He starts banging his head against the door
It opens up recent wounds
From his friends the Hoodies
He shits in the corner
And rubs it all over the wall

He hasn't pissed for hours
He is so wound up
He lets go in his pants
And sings a song of Liberty
For Blacks and Paks and Jocks

He doesn't know where that came from
But it amuses the older cops
Who are congregating at the spectacle
"Idi Amin the most amazing Scotsman in Africa"
The cops are in hysterics of laughter
He is now extremely agitated (mad)

The Doctor and nurse arrive
He has an amazing conversation with them
Things are finally settled
They would take him to a safe place
The cops escort him to the hospital
In the flying squad van

It is a jovial affair
He likes these guys
They even show him a Smith and Wesson revolver
They duly arrive at the hospital
He is handcuffed for appearances they say.

He is greeted by four big male nurses
They appear to have forked tongues
And hyena like eyes
The handcuffs are taken off
The cops disappear
His mates have deserted him
He feels betrayed

He can see an attractive female nurse in the background
She is holding a syringe
Behind her is a pink room
He decides she is the famous prostitute
Like in the Book of Revelation
"We've got something to calm you down" she says
Her hair turns into snakes
"Not fuckin likely, bitch"
Suddenly he is grabbed
And roughly held down
    he screams for his cop mates
He struggles but to no avail

Suddenly a white hot stab in the buttock
They seem to hold him down forever
He can't breathe
A Knee behind the neck

The angels from hell without their bikes
The pink room starts to swim
It feels like barbed wire is coursing through his veins.

(Read the rest slow)

He is in hell
They let him go and the door slams shut
Where are you, God?
He stumbles and crawls around
He spots a camera in the ceiling
He gives it the bird
He notices a mattress and horse blanket
And a stainless steel toilet in the corner
He screams
He screams again
"King Baby"
He bangs the door with head and feet
Blood everywhere
He sits still
He decides he is a Foreign Legionnaire
He needs a uniform
He spies the mattress
And starts tearing the cover into strips
First the kepi hat
This keeps him busy
"The bastards aren't breaking me" he thinks
The effects of the injection are working
He dribbles and stumbles and gropes
But he is still racing inside
Keep making uniform
Keep busy
Don't give up!
Suddenly the door clangs open
The nurses escort him out
They think he is making a rope
Out onto the ward
He crawls along the floor groping the wall

Dribbling and drooling.
He feels a presence
He looks up
A tattooed face and a gappy grin
"Who are you?" he dribbles
"Napoleon, Bro – President of the Mongolian Mongrel Mob.
Who are you, Bro?"
"He, Shamanic Irish Monk of Aotearoa"
"Cher, He. Want a smoke?"
"Cheers, Bro".

The hours and then the days go by
More Largactil injections
He chain smokes, even rolling up butts.
The skin peels off his tongue
They give him Cogentin for the side effects
Now he can't see properly
Napoleon says "You gotta act, Bro!"
The days roll on
No sleep
Just more Largactil
He abuses the nurses
More Largactil
Napoleon says "You gotta act, Bro!"
He wants to sit down
But when he does he wants to get up
Catch 22

Napoleon makes a decision
He is now the Black Power adviser to Vladimir Putin
"He" sticks with his Shamanic Irish Monk thing
He buys a carton of Lucky Strikes
Chain smoking like a Shaman with PTSD
They, the doctors you don't see, change his medication to Melleril
Plus introducing Lithium
They don't stop his high.
Now he just tries to climb the walls
Instead of crawling on the floor
A big lion in a small cage.

Napoleon introduces him to some of the others
They all seem to play pool and table tennis
"How do they do that on this shit?"
Napoleon says "look like you behave
And they reduce your medication
So you play table tennis and get ground parole".
He says, "How do I do that?"
"Act normal, Bro"
The penny drops.
"I couldn't conquer Europe without acting, Bro".
Napoleon introduces He to Amundo and Skonson
Skonson models himself on the Joker in a pack of cards
"He's been here 2 years now, Bro"
Skonson swings an 8 ball on a piece of flax.
Amundo uses a single crutch due to an undiagnosed hip complaint
And claims to be a Warlock
"Weirdos – Amundo has been here 18 months
They act normal, Bro".
He says "What about you, Napoleon?"
"Been here 3 years, Bro."
"Why?"
"I act normal"
Oh! Catch 22, One flew over the cuckoo nest

This is fun
These guys have connections
They have Thai Buddha supplied by one of the nurses
They run the OT department
They have ground parole
They act normal
The penny was still dropping
Only as far as to why they have been in so long

He started acting normal
He got ground parole
He went to OT with his new mates
He smoked Thai Buddha with some of the nurses
He discussed Irish Monasticism with his friends

They took him seriously
They said "you just don't talk about that stuff with plebs
And nurses"

He liked his new world – sort of
He was six weeks in now
He knew he had to get out sometime
The BMW was repossessed
He had no job
And the flat was gone
This scared him.

He could stay here
On ground parole he saw some sights
Disturbing sights
The results of modern society
Mostly due to in-breeding
The retarded infant villa had a barbed wire security fence
To keep the paedophile patients out
You couldn't go for a swim for two reasons
Retards pissed and shit in the pool
And retard perverts masturbated while watching you have a swim.

Without dope and medication this place would be hell.
Everybody is nuts, including the staff
Especially the staff
No wonder the nurses do drugs and party on time off
Manic depression isn't fun
You just gotta act normal.
Why have Napoleon, Amundo and Skonson been in so long?
Cos they are scared of normal people when they get out

Is Bi Polar due to in-breeding?
No
But in-breeding is a lack of self-control
Seemingly normal people have no self-control
Some of the nurses have none
Some cops

Some politicians and priests
Some TV preachers
Some people in the UN
Some nightclub patrons and hoodies
Manic Depressives who don't take Lithium
I.e. Napoleon and Alexander the Great
They all met with a bad end

He decided self-control was where it's at
Acting normal doesn't cut it, he thought
Otherwise you only stay where you are
Like Napoleon, Amundo and Skonson

It wasn't long before he got out
He got a job as a builder's labourer
Saved up a bit and bought some tools
And went back to his trade
He reconciled with Cindy
They married and had 4 kids
He studied Irish and American Indian history
Cindy thought he was nuts
She kept him in line
Only when she thought he was losing his self-control
She was glad he was not normal.

REDEMPTION

Jesus might one day, take your blues away,
In the meantime you will have to live with them.
And he will help you in that respect,
Maybe you will make friends with the blues,
It's called paying your dues.

You can live on credit only for so long,
Then comes the day to pay it all back.
Don't expect easy terms.
Because the loan shark you borrowed off,
Demands pretty high interest rates.

   That's the Blues.

Jesus will clear your debts,
Then you will start getting savvy.
You'll start working real hard,
And put some money away in his bank.
You'll live within your means.

   It's not money I'm talking about.

Life is a bit like a ledger.
An account book if you like.
The time will come at the end,
To settle your accounts.
What if you are in the red?

   Scary aye?

You are back to the loan shark.
Who is he?
Everybody at some stage in life,
Goes to the loan shark.
He offers easy credit.

THE HAPPINESS HILL

I psych myself up the for the run
Put my shoes on for to go
I start moving up that road
Reach the gate and there's my hill
I put my head down and arse up
Breathing hard I start to climb
I pause at different points
Admire the view and see where I've been
Man this is hard, could stop anytime.
Steeper stuff to come, I must keep going
Got to get to the lookout
All cares will be gone on the top of my world
Lungs are burning on this one to one slope
I stop to listen to a distinctive crack
The old Billy goats having a fight
I scramble through scrub and fallen pines
Nearly there, I go through the gorse tunnel
Up through my hidden track
Stepping quietly and always aware
Just like jungle training years ago
And what do I see looking at me?
"Who the hell are you", is his look
Yes, twenty feet away a forty pound pig
And three of his busy mates
Two take off and two are too busy
Dumb pigs
I get to the lookout at a thousand feet
Put on my swani and have a smoke
The view is good and I've worked hard
And I'm so bloody happy on my hill
Now I've got to go down
Where I mostly am
Where I live
With them
People
And I've got to find happiness there.

PART IX

ROOTS

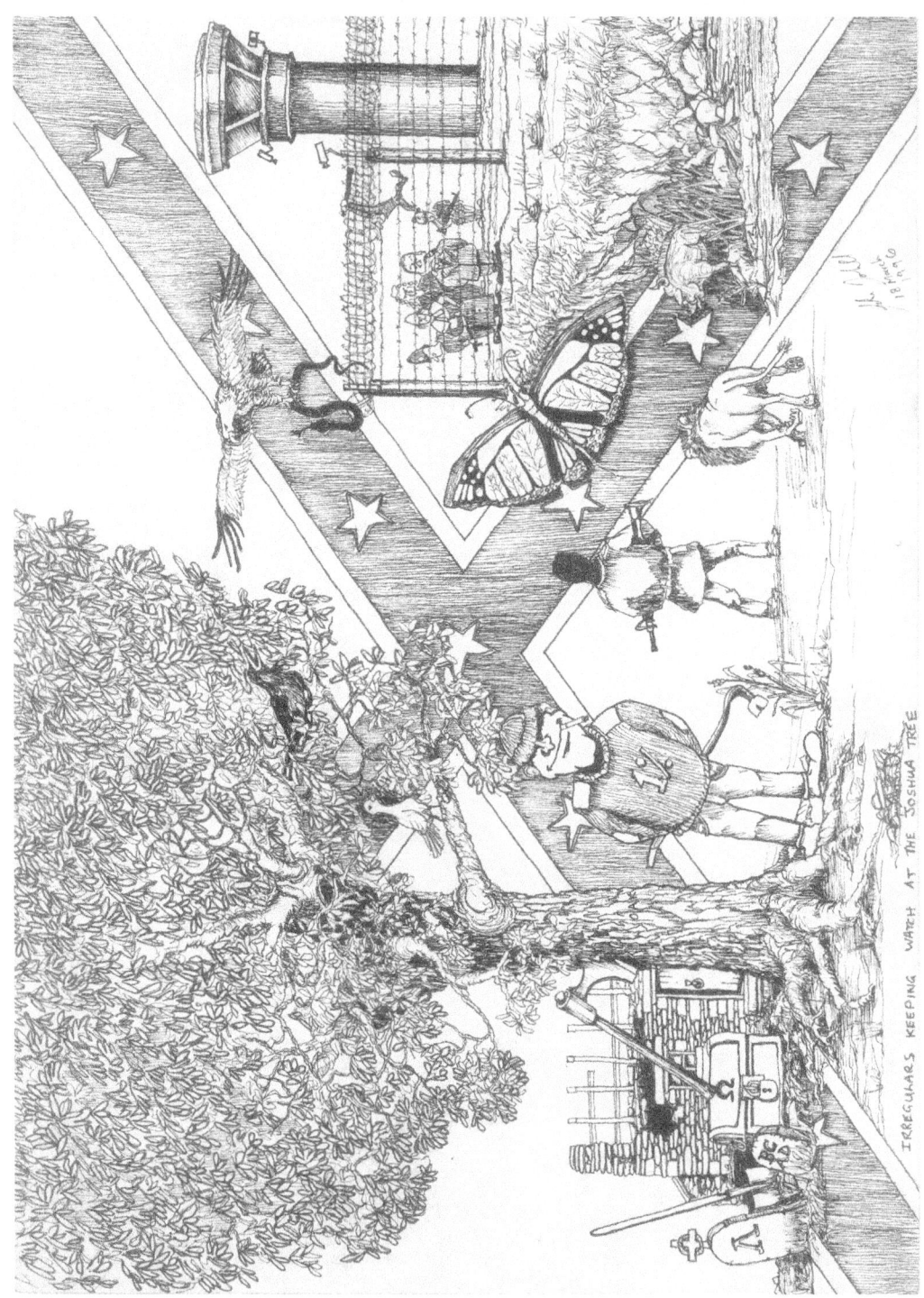

Irregulars keeping watch at the Joshua Tree

THE DRUM: PULSE OF MY HEART

Drumbeat, pounding in my mind
Heartbeat, drumbeat in my blood
My Spirit rises high above
It burrows deep down below
I run through time and space
Watching, listening, questing
I see great wonders and Truth
They are mine for my passage
On my shoulders a Rook and a Dove
And treading softly beside me
Are the Lion and Boar
And an angel from above.

I am a singer of the moon
Brother of the drum
The oak, ash and thorn I see
The Tuatha of times long gone
I shake the fenian branch
All is quiet in my mind
I listen .....
To those ancient men, they are me
To the music of the Father in Heaven
To the voices of all creatures
To the Spirit and the Son
And the spirit of the land
I ride the voice of that drum.

I am on my journey to being
Who and what I am
As the fire leaps and the water flows
As the earth breathes and the air swirls
So do I
MY FATHER IS THE DRUMBEAT AND HEARTBEAT
HE IS THE SONG OF MY SOUL!

"LE CROGACHT AGUS DILSEACHT"
(Hunger Striker Conversation)

"Glainne ar croidghe neart neag beart derir ar mbhriathi."
"Ar mhaith leat deoch uisce?"
"Ba mhaith".
"Lean ar aghaidh, ta a lan uisce san ait seo".
"Cad a shilealearn tu faoi sin?"
"Na bac, Lean ar aghaidh".
"Misa ta aun"
"Cade mar ata tu?"
"Nilim romh dhona, agus tu fein?"
"Ta me go hiontach: ta daoine eile anseo?"
"Teastaionn uatha caint leat".
"Failte!"
"Beannacht De ort agus bi curamach".
"Lean ar aghaidh, Tiocfaidh ar la!"

R.I.P. Bobby Sands

TUATHAL TEACHTMAIR

It is a fine Northumbrian day
Springtime in the Roman month of May
You whistle and sing to yourself
While your two granddaughters are at play
You are in an oak grove to select
And pick new shoots and herbs
For use in your healing art, kept secret
Handed down from long ago to today.

Suddenly the children yelp, you hear a galloping horse
"Look Nana, it's a wild man from far away" a warrior approaches riding
    very hard
Helmet and shield, with a kilt of strange design
Blood dripping from wounds and blade.

He reigns in his dark chestnut horse
And he looks you over severe
He reverses his sword holding by blade
A gesture of parley is being made
Blue woad covers his face, he has a fiery stare
Pointing pommel straight at you
Not shifting his mesmeric glare.

He states in accent strange, with imperious tone
"You are a Celt of healing skills" the girls relax, instant like for this man
"I'm not sure about the first, but yes to the second"
"Are you finished with your gathering?" he asks.
"Not quite" you say, with chin held high.
"Send a sprat for water, I thirst" he commands.
The dark haired one runs off, despite your objection.
The light haired one views the man with interest.

On close inspection, wounds found not serious
Most of the blood is not his
Just incidental scratches and cuts
You tend these, as your wont

Water fetched and drank, children do hover
"How many of ours did your raiders slay?"
"Thrice two or thereabouts I would say."
You start to shake and cry
He says to allay your distress in reply
"Only the Saxon born, black blooded and foul."
"Oh, thank the mighty Cernahnos!" you breathe
"DON'T SPEAK OF COURRUPT DIETYS' IN MY PRESENCE!"
The blue painted warrior does roar.
You protest like only a woman can
But before you utter a foul curse
He raises oaken shield and sword
But before you a mighty Lion does roar
Crested by a resolute Boar.

"By the tribes and the Land you'll no longer live under tainted hand.
Come now walk with these totems
The most powerful of my fair land".
"Where is this fair land then?" you churlishly ask
But your inquiry is deftly ignored
"Never mind, your family are safe,"
"They have your aspects and the dark hair"
"Oh thank you blue faced man," you primly reply
"What is your name, if I may be so bold", you ask.
"I am the TUATHAL" he does shyly reply.
"A strange and mysterious name! I might say".
"I just showed it to you, fixed on my shield!"
"Then you must have a fine weapon to wield!"
"Enough, get on the horse the three of you!"
You reach your village about midday
Near the gates are six headless bodies
Where they had fallen, did they lay
Food for the crows
Men at arms, of Saxon overlord
The rest had fled not tarrying where
Fierce wild men from out of the west.
Had come causing them great fear.
"Don't fret woman, your men are safe

They did not run, weaponless as they were
You will come with us, collect what you need."

Then you see a woman standing there
She is tall, with pale skin and long black hair
Wearing a sword like the men
A "Harridan", the Romans called them of old
Fierce and yet beautiful, like stories told.
She appraises you with a knowing stare
"It's not from these men you need to fear,
Your slave masters have scuttled off,
We are taking you to a land so fair,
You'll be treated well, there's a place for you,
Cousins of the Gael, hold your heads high".

You feel more at ease under her hard stare
"Lady I thank you, for your kind mercy"
She replies sternly "A sister of mine needs not beg apology! .
These men are your brothers and we are kin,
I am Moya of Glendalough
Freedom you now have, this is your chance
Take what is yours, or be a slave."

The children seem not perturbed at all
Somewhat confused are their Fathers and Uncles
Your daughters fear what the future holds
Tuathals men, The Niall and Cormac the Seer
Fit the fathers and uncles with weapon and shield
Telling of obligation and choices they have
Of following cruel "protector" or going with them
In the direction of the "setting sun".

Down at the shore you embark on the boats
Sailing west to the Land of Legends told
Sailing over night, navigation by strange means, the stars,
A method learnt from Milesian forefathers, long ago
Taught to them by a Semitic people
Whom with they had tarried with a while
When in mercenary service of the Pharaoh Cingris

Aaron, being the leader of these twelve tribes
He had healed their Chieftain of a fatal snakebite
Using but a Rod and Staff
Aaron prophesied their Chieftain would one day find
A forested, serpent free Island Land
This is a tale Moya did relate.

On the dawn of the next day
That is what you see before you
A beautiful green forested land
The boat lands, all disembark-without fuss
Greetings are made and boasts are recited
Your company is fed, hospitality unimagined
Your men are satired straight off of course
Foreigners with no device or kilt
But treated as clan never the less
Straight into talk of horses and cattle
And inquired of any trade or skill
Your progeny immediately make friends
Playing with wolf and hounds, scaring the cats
The light haired one is talking to a Shannachie
He tells her tales of the other world and the like
The dark-haired one bosses hound and cattle beast
And soon is riding a pony around.

Your Sons in law join in all the revels
Sons as well inquiring of the fishing
Sparring, spear throwing and horse racing
The customs and language are quite baffling
But you somehow feel at home
Your family all feel very welcome
A festival is taking place, called a "feis"(fesh)
There is a lot of trade going on
Works of gold and silver, smithed to high degree
Traded for ordinary items, though valued equally
Not a coin anywhere to be seen
With tyrants head on it stamped
The music and dance is beyond compare.

Suddenly you feel a presence
You turn to see the man Tuathal
He stands there but now he looks changed
A wild eyed warrior he is no more
His kilt now brooched, a fine cloak he wears
Luna and torc of gold, silver belt and sword
Hair braided, on his head a band of red gold
But eyes that see a road paved with pain
Druids and strange "Christ priests" are in train.

"Come with me woman, I am in need of your Art"
All fall silent as you with them part.
You come soon to a small hill on the plain of Meath
Tuathal stops and points to it.
The sun is setting, Tuathal quietly speaks.
"I am TUATHAL TEACHTMAIR and I am chosen
From a council of all the Chieftains of Erin.
That hill is Tara, my betrothed
My heart, My pulse, My obligation,
Without my marriage to her there is no life.
My relationship with her and the Christ,
And the ways of the Oak
Are free for my passage."

"But the only son born of me was stolen
By the dragon people we rescued you from.
I am at peace with my own destiny.
What is about to happen is proof of that
And I will face it, come what be
I have no problem with it
But because of the separation
Being torn from my own flesh and blood
A sacrifice for to keep the Faith.
I've had my soul ripped apart
The Father will set it right one day
So these priests here do say
But you can heal me now
While I'm still in this body

The pain is with me every day
You are like the "Drui-een
Flying this way and that about the oak".

They wait in the darkness till morning
Just before first light
You watch mystified as the company enter the hill
Through a cave like entrance, so old
You are motioned to stay away
There is silence, the Christ men don't enter
Minutes go by, there is total silence
Then something happens,
The hairs stand up on your neck
Your whole body does zing
The rising sun's light pierces the entrance
There is total stillness all around

Suddenly you hear an ungodly scream
A cry of ecstasy and agonized pain
From deep in the earth and up through your bones
Caused by a great and ancient power
Now more than just the sun's light
But another emanates from within the entrance
You feel what has happened
But you will never dare
To put what you witness
To words of the mouth
That would be sacrilege
There is a curse on those who steal what is not theirs.
Ancient mysteries must be left
To the rightful inheritors
If they ever should come to know

The sun rises, morning has broken
Silence has reigned seemingly for a long time
The company comes out of the Mound
Tuathal is being carried by the Druids
He is semi-conscious, exhausted and in pain

The Christ Men start praying "The Prayer"
They seem to understand what has happened
You do too, but then you never will
The Druids carry Tuathal to you
He says to you "I am destiny, I now have a wife."
You are baffled, concerned for the man's physical state.
"Heal me now woman, Wren of the Oak,
For I must still live in this world"
"I don't know what to do" you say
"It's not what your mind knows, Drui-een,
The spirit of your Art will show you,
It's about being what you are."
"What is it that I am?"
"You are – that is what you know."
"I will try to be."
"Thank you." says he.

The company return to the Tuatha
A great Bonfire is lit
Other fires spring up in the distance
The Feis of Tara has again taken place
The Stone of Fal has once again cried out
Tuathal is now under obligation, Faoi gheasa,
He must protect the people and make peace
Between the provinces and the Septs
He must serve God, Three in One
He knows Christ is his brother,
He must be sure the old ways of the oak survive

The High King asks you casually
"Pray tell woman, what is your name?"

CHEIFTAN OF THE GLEN (ADAPTED FROM MO GHILE MEAR)

The Tanist with his fierce fighting men
Roared down from out of the glen
Upon the English holding the Pale
Trapping them in the fen.
These men of the Lion and Boar, the Gael
Did not savour this filthy battle
But knowing the women and children
Were the dirty Hun's ultimate prey
Left no choice but to defend
And keep proud independence assured
For just another day
Na Ghile Mear, a chuisle, mo chroi

Greif and pain are all the women know
Their hearts sore, their tears do flow
Looking on proudly, seeing the men go
No word is written of them more.
Story and lesson handed down
To today from Mum to child
Deeds of Fathers not realised
Till son goes through the same
Playing centuries old cruel game
Of proud and gallant Chevalier
High born Scions of brave men past
Fiery blades engaged to weild
Irish Creed and the Father shield
Always braving the bravest on the field
Mo Ghile Mear, a chuisle, mo chroi.

We sing their praise our sweet harps play
And proudly toast their noble fame
Don't spare a thought, have conscience clear
Stand your ground
You'll be honoured with strength and length of days
So keep the faith and be brave.

SEAN O'TUATHAIL

Today just like then when
Our forebears gave up land and life
Staying faithful to the way
We stand against the same today
Beast craving for your strong spirit
That he can never have
Conquering the world
Destroying peoples and ways of life
Who were happy living in God's grace.

Be like those men of the Glen
They fought the fight to the grave
All but wiped from histories books
Only Victor's lies put down
Handed to descendents to feel shame,
We suffer under the same foe still
Insidiously entrenched in our laws and religion.

Look around and compare
Like that wasp in the bee's nest there
And don't forget what you're up against
Like in the Dire Straits song
He's very big and he's very strong
Been ruling the world for too bloody long
Stand your ground, soul and heart
Don't forget you're in the right.
Despite all the beasts power and might
He will never win the ultimate fight.

(for the Ui Tuathail and the fighting Irish)

EMERALD AND GOLD

I was lying on the lounge floor,
Cat Stevens on the headphones
"Where do the children play?" sung he
Good music, staring at the ceiling
    Drifting from thought to dream
    Then gradually or so it did seem
The white of the ceiling did pulse
Radiating in circular bands
Rippling out from emerald to gold
My eyes did water at the sight
Like when you look too long at the sun
I must say I got a bit of a fright
    But not the kind that comes from fear.

Maybe I had just hallucinated
Could of, I spose, that's for you to decide
Who cares? This was real for me
It was my spirit doing the seeing
I also heard a soothing voice
Calming my upset and angry soul
Caused by the days unfolding events
    Me being helpless to do much about them
As I live on the Far Side of the World
Far from the land my forbears were forced to leave
But a land I always regard as Home.

The voice, He told me not to worry at all
The Archangel Michael with bright sword at hand
Was guarding the Garvaghy Road
From the senseless Lambeg thumping mobs
Complete with their sashes and silly hats
    Marching boys frightening women and kids
Fire, rape and pitchfork their "proud" legacies
Lunatic bandsmen of an idiot creed
Cromwell and Dutchman King Billy their heroes
Perversion of Truth their desperate need.

SEAN O'TUATHAIL

Even more assuring, the man in white said
Was the fact that the Advocate in His mercy
Had rescued three of His innocent ones
Murdered by some of their neighbours
Attempting to burn out "filthy Taigs"
Whose only crime was to live on a Protestant Street
Part of Most Reverend Paisley's stronghold
Burned alive while they slept in bed
By proud defenders of Queen and "Faith".
This is what the man in white told
The boys had been taken to Paradise
A place that is coloured all Emerald and Gold.

So don't worry about injustice and hard times
The strong will be made weak in the end
Keep the Faith and stick to your guns
The tyrant always hangs himself you know
With his own whip he will swing.

You don't have to forgive the bastards either
But they will try to make you forget
Saying it wasn't their fault, just a crazy few
Not till they get down on their knees
And confess their trespass and are contrite
Hold your "thirty two cals" to their heads
Look at eight hundred years of murder
And wonder if you should forgive
Ask the Archangel Michael
He will tell you when and where
To do what you want as a man to do.

OGLAIGH NA n ERRIAN

2320 13 July 1998 "Marching Season"

THE BLACK EYE PENAL – POGUE MAHONE

He was a clansman and a cattle farmer
He watched as evil men came
He didn't know they were at the time
But he welcomed them according to his people's laws of hospitality
They came with promises and treaties
Also with a thick black Book
With this they came up with a list of do's and don'ts
They backed it up with sword and musket
The clansmen got nervous.

Overnight the evil men were everywhere
Smashing statues and altars in the people's churches
They didn't stop there, they hunted the Priests
And sent them into hiding
If caught they were tortured and killed.
But worse, they were repossessing land
That wasn't theirs in the first place
Because of documents drawn up on their paper
The clansman was about to become a Black Eye Penal.
The commanding officer of the evil men
Was over enamoured with the clansman's sister
She refused him, as was her right
This humiliated the Commander
She was hung on a gibbet.

This enraged the men of the Sept
They rose up against their oppressors
Every man fought but to no avail
Most were killed the rest were scattered.
The evil men turned on the women and children
They pitchforked the babies and raped the women
All in the name of God.

The evil men now had possession of the land
The people had nowhere to run or hide
But the evil men needed workers

The people had to work for them and rent their own land
But they worshipped in secret
And living secure in the knowledge
That they were in the right.
They lived, not as well as in the past
But they lived in hope.

They were second class citizens in their own land
This was to last for generations
But they never lost hope
And they never lost their faith in their God
They remained brave and faithful
They got treated like Black Eye Penals
They waited
The evil men profited
These men felt justified by their black Book
The Black Eye Penals just survived
Generations later they suffered a great famine
And a round of evictions.

But one Black eye Penal survived this.
Some years later
He became a member of the Constabulary for a while.
He gained passage to Victoria, Australia
He served two years there as a mounted constable.
He was discharged on the twelfth of June 1861,
He was one free Black Eye Penal
He decided to search for gold
He delved in New South Wales.

He was a big man, six foot with grey eyes
But he always remembered he was a Black eye Penal
He knew he belonged to a great Sept
He knew who he was and he had honour
But he was well dressed in humility
He knew no evil men could take that away.

His search for gold took him to New Zealand
First the West Coast beaches, then the Dunstan

He staked a claim near Ophir
But then he ran into the Browns.
The Browns jumped his claim,
Some sleight of hand with the pegs they say.

There was a heated discourse outside the Post Office
The Black Eye Penal drew his cap and ball colt
The matter was sorted out.
After this, he went back to Victoria via Dunedin
Staying with relations en route
He purchased a "selection" at Campaspe and settled
He farmed the 300 acres and was content
He was known for his "manly and kindly attributes"
He was also known as a friend of the Kellys

The Black Eye Penal had a son, among others,
Of the same name and stature
Of the same nature, straight and true
An axeman that beat all comers.
He made his way to the Dunstan in 1905
After some time logging in Tasmania
He settled and married a beautiful woman named Mary Ethel
They lived through two World wars and a Depression
They had seventeen children who all survived
The last one born in 1932.

This son was a musterer, Sparky and Otago rugby player
He was a bit of a lad and could play the piano well
He liked a beer but you had to watch him on whisky
He married a beautiful woman named Kathleen Isobel in 1961.
They had nine children over the ensuing years
When he drank whisky he would tell me about the Black eye Penals
The whole story, it made me frightened and angry
I learned to hate, but that was my fault
All dad wanted me to know was the truth
In his own way.

I hope my son will learn the truth without hating
Because evil men have you right where they want you

If you hate
Hate rots your heart
And a rotten heart is prone to evil
Then you become an evil man
What's the point in that?

PART X

UISCE FAOI THALAMH

FAITH

FROM GO TO WOE

Mankind was given, Free
Just on one condition
The marvel of paradise
There between the rivers
In the garden of Eden
Instructed not to swipe
The juicy forbidden fruit
From the tree
Right there in the middle
Ishshah was wholly deceived
By the wily dragon crawling
She picked it with a pluck
Persuading Ish to bite
What was this tasty crop?
You have always wondered
Knowledge of good and evil?
Power over life and death?
I don't really know
Not having been there
But you can be sure it was wrong
Not ours to plunder and steal.
We have huge powers of thought
And free will given as a gift
Being made in God's image
All his animal kingdom
Seem so bloody savage
Yet they don't carry the burden
Of original legacy foul
This separates us from them
"Mankind" and "To Live" banished
To the wild country rugged
Made to feel shame
Fending for themselves in the dirt
Childbirth in extreme pain
Murdering and stealing
Right to the present time

Only fleeting peace of mind
Brief "Paradise" for bloodstained few
One man's wealth and riches
Is slavery for multitudes
Striving for futile glimpse
Of Divine Glory
Soon smashed down hard
By angry Amen blade
Cain is just a name you think?
Oh no! It means to acquire
Murdering son of a bitch!
Indians and Abos still Abel!
Let's skip some millenniums here, OK?
Spreading all over the globe today
Amoral, money crazed people
Now turning to genetics and cloning
Propagation of bizarre new fruits
Knowledge of Life and Death, Good and Evil
The Result, a disastrous abomination
Complete with sex change and clown hat!
To replace a shunned Almighty Father
But they still find much power
In the vain use of His name
To me it's all madness and shame
We won't listen to the Begotten One
Adam now speeding to the brink
The Hand of Love will wipe the slate clean
But only for those who turn their backs
On the ways of the hidden killer
This thing hasn't revealed himself yet
Only through unknowing Captains and Kings
Always sneaking in dreams and thoughts
His name is in a number
Many fools have tried to divine
But obvious to those of us
Who don't draw on our own store
Soon you won't be able to buy
Even a pack of twenty's

Without the invisible cyber coin!
(Please take time to understand!)
What of us Paddy Mick Catholics?
With the responsibility we carry
Peter's confirmation mark so sacred
Rubbed on our foreheads
Worse for us who turn away
Already having been saved
Don't worry over this, you prods
It doesn't really matter!
It's one of ours that did
Slide the condom over the Ocean Star at Te Papa!
Don't be frightened, Black Sheep
Stick with your loving friend
Who gave his bleeding heart
To take the load off you
Trust in Him one hundred percent
Before Him death departs
And dread fear evaporates
Going up in smoke
Be a true one percenter
Give ninety nine to friends
Leave the other one behind
Six foot under, when you leave
And eternal peace you might find
Dirt to Dirt, Ash to Ash

FROM EAST TO WEST (A PEARL TO THE SWINE)

Wondering about the point?
How you got here,
Where you are going?
Is your faith being shaken
By all the shit going down?
Doing the following exercise
May get you back on the road.

Here goes, now bear with me
Go down to the beach.
If you are in jail, or too far away,
Use your imagination
To take you.
If you haven't got one,
No use going further with me.
I'm sure there is someone itching
To get on in there
And make use of that empty space.
After all, what use is a computer
With no one to punch the keys?

Getting back to the point,
Here is what you do.
Find somewhere peaceful and quiet.
If you go in the evening,
Be sure the moon is full.
Also go once again at sunrise or sunset,
Depending which way you face.
Be sure that you are
On a rising tide.
Not being merely academic,
But an exercise of experience.

Be in a good state of mind.
At peace, being the key.

Why not say a prayer?
If you are so heathen
That you can't remember
Recite something in your mind,
Maybe one of the following;
Like Baa, Baa, Black Sheep,
Or Mary had a Little Lamb.
Don't smoke any dope,
Or drink any whiskey.

Even having a beer
Or taking other drugs
Will blur and muddle your mind.
You will need a clear head.

Right! Where were we?
Oh yeah, that's right.
You have got to the beach,
The sun is setting or rising,
It's late April or early May.
Or late September or early October.
You don't have to understand,
Just do it.
A revelation will come,
Then again it might not.
A cup that's full
Can't have any more added.

Ok, stand where the water meets the land,
Feet wet, but also in the sand.
Feel the wind on your face,
Oh yeah, take your shoes off first.
Now, it's handy if you are a smoker,
Because you need a flame.
Light your smoke and chill out.
Look around, pull your head out
From up your arse
If things are that bad.

Smell the fresh air,
Enjoy that smoke.

In case you haven't already realised,
You are now standing on the Earth,
Soaking in the Water,
Feeling the Air,
And breathing (dare I say) Fire.

These are the four elements,
The elements of Mother Nature,
Who gave birth to you,
Your physical body.
Look at the sun,
Giving life to the Mother
So that she may be fertile
And produce food for her children,
The giver of life,
The marker of the seasons.

Look at the moon,
Its energy a pale reflection,
Of the power of the sun.
Controller of the tides (moods and emotions).
Giving women a rest,
Time to recuperate from the rigours of their work.
Sun and Moon, indicators of Festivals and Feasts.

Think of the stars,
Lights to see the way by,
When the sky Father is asleep,
Giving his wife a rest.
Stars are a measure of time,
Future and past.
Look at the Universe,
Wow, how big!
And out beyond that?
The Creator of it all.

Have another smoke.
Pick up a grain of sand,
Think of it as our planet
And all it contains.
How many more on the beach?
Take it all in.
Look North then South,
Look East then West.
Where do these directions come from?
Where do they go?
How is it all held together?
Does it matter?

Why do we hurt our Mother so?
Why do we dishonour Our Father?
Is it ours to question why?
Or are we just part of a big game?
Do you think you could count
How many grains of sand there are?
Or how many stars there are?
The sum of all mankind's achievement,
All his wisdom and knowledge,
Is as that grain of sand.
God knows – He is the rest.
He is and He was,
And always will be.

And we think we know better,
I don't think so.

Have another smoke.
The water is up to your waist.
Look at the sun again,
That is just one of the stars.
You can't look at it for long,
It is too bright.
A small measure of God's brilliance,
That is power.

Who is more powerful?
Mankind or God?
Go find a high place.
Think about what you have done.
After doing this, say:

Our Father who art in Heaven
Hallowed be Thy Name
Thy kingdom come......

1500 21 June 1998
GR 027 322 914
173° 16'N 41°17'S

BENAI ELOHIM
(The Tower of Babel)

One of the greatest mysteries,
The whereabouts of the Gateway of the God;
Said to be on a plain in the land of Shinar.
A story handed down from before history.
The folly of a great hunter, King Nimrod.
An open secret if you read
What the scribe says in parable told.
Maybe a story based on real events,
Man getting too big for his boots,
In context of our modern times
We still behave the same,
Sky and Eiffel, World Trade Centre,
Monuments to our vanity, to name but a few.

And now some have the need
To prove this event happened.
It was the first time, that's the point, don't you see?
Bible delvers use archaeological methods
And pseudo religious comparisons,
With large semi academic twit brains.
Shows a lack of faith, I reckon.
What spirit guides these wasters of time?

Who gives a damn when, where or if
This city and tower were built?
Or whether Saddam dug it up?
If you have the Spirit helping you read,
The message stands out clear;
Time and place are not important;
The story is repeated over and over
Like all the other chapters and verses;
For reception in the heart
Not the cluttered brain.

SEAN O'TUATHAIL

It's understanding between brother and race.
That God took away, due to disgrace.
Caused by deviant behaviour that man did stoop to,
In the attempt to reach the heights
Required to get to the gates
Of the celestial realm he thinks is in the sky
Where God and court are thought to rule.
Our spaceships haven't reached there yet,
But you can be sure heaven is there,
And here and everywhere, just not where you "think".

Have a look around, see history and current events,
Read fiction and the so called facts.
How come we can't get our shit together?
Make a happy world for the kids?
No, we fight and argue, won't understand each other
Whether at home, work or on the campus,
Languages of all kinds abound.
Even in your insular protected circle,
Nothing but "babble".

So don't come to me with your pointing finger,
Condemning Saddam, the Arabs and half the human race
It's people like you, too, the Father has punished,
For assuming you'll have exclusive audience.
Like Cain being jealous, murdering your brother,
Attempting to acquire what his behaviour didn't warrant.
You pollute the sanctuary that you guard,
You wage war with your lying blasphemy,
You still think it's someone else I speak of.
Don't you?

Is the life you have made for yourself
Built from fired bricks and mortar of pitch
Easily smashed and burnt?
Or is the life you have made for yourself
Built of solid rocks, fitted tight?

Hard to bring down and easy to defend.

With the first way of life you will always have to run
And be forced to toe the line;
Always living in fear, furtive and insecure.
But with second way I've mentioned,
There is always a fortified place,
No "landlord" and "taxman" threatening space,
Book inside not full of rules redundant.
A place of refuge, safe from attack and abuse,
No storm can break it or fire burn it.

The first is built on sand
The second on a rock called "Cephas" in Greek
In one, house rules narrow, blinkered and bleak;
The other is universal, taking in all travellers,
Three housekeepers – but only One;
Only two house rules, even children understand
One guiding charter and first aid kit.
Many rooms, a guardian for each bed;
Every feature set in Ancient Rock.
No keys to the many gates are needed,
Just say the word, be contrite for sin,
And you will be let in.

Go away if you like, discover life's wonders
Come back any time, with it's lessons
You'll be given, for your travels,
A bag to sustain you on your road
And a map to find your way back
Benai Elohim.

DESCENT NOT EVOLUTION — Ariel and the primeval one.

GUNNA – "LIKE A THIEF"

Wadda ya gunna do, when the shit hits
    the fan?
Wadda ya gunna do, about getting bread
    milk and meat?
The shops will all be looted, windows smashed
    gutted and burnt out?
And how will you withdraw your cash from
    a bank that's closed?
Computer systems and the ATMs will all
    have long since crashed
They are always the first ones to leave, Telecom will
    be a joke
There will be fist fights at the Gas Stations,
    maybe you'll have to walk.

Wadda ya gunna do? Aye!
When your quarter acre paradise
Gets caught in the crossfire?
But the police are all dead
And the Army is protecting parliament
There are gangs and factions about,
Coloured black, white, red and blue.
Sorry mate, you're gunna have to choose
Because you don't have the means to protect
Your wife, kids and property all on your own.
Hah! Wadda ya gunna do?

Hey look, it's that twenty year old loser
That you in the past so much despised
You wrote letters to the editor then
Now he's packing an S.L.R.
God knows where he got it from
In your trust of the government,
You handed yours in, you fool!
The little bastard is pointing it at you

Eyeing your daughters with mischievous grin
What the hell are ya gunna do?!!

The little shit's faction is holding this turf
At the moment they are the law
You will have to toe the line now.
You never thought you would see the day
When the rule of law no longer holds sway.
Society has dishonoured it's young for so long
And now you are paying the price
For the system's iniquity
The system you supported, by the way.

What-are-you-going-to-do? Hmmm
Hah! You say you did your bit
But you handed over social responsibility
And your fat arse too
You wiped your hands clean, not good enough,
Look where it's got you now
There is no rationalising anymore
Not while you're looking down the barrel of a gun, aye!
You silly bastard, there's no help on the way.
What are you going to do?
Where did it all start?
Bear with me, I'll try to explain.

Here you are back in the present
Thinking that your past and history in general
Has no meaning or bearing on the now
Or you would not be sitting in this pew
All is swept under the carpet you think
Not very comfortable with what you hear
Doesn't seem relevant anymore
But it's only an hour of the week
A chance to show off the Porsche
What better way than at church
All your friends are there too
Well. What's a man to do?

What's the minister on about anyway?
You idly ask yourself, peeking at your watch.
You wonder which way he voted at the synod
And whether he likes wine too much
Or if he's one of them that is gay
A business opportunity, you think
You fiddle impatiently with your Rotary pin
Exchange Masonic nods and winks with your "Brothers"
Using all 43 Goat Rider signals
Life is pretty damn sweet right now
Your money is working on the market
The Condom Business is booming
What else does one have to do?

You can't really stomach the sermon though
"Thief in the night" and Gospel of John
Even if it's half-heartedly recited
From watered down Protestant dogma
You might suggest later he tones things down
A word in the ear at next Lodge or Parish meeting
Maybe hint where his funding is coming from
Sometimes he really strikes a nerve
Like the one this writer might be striking now.
Normally it all fits in so well
With the way you choose to live your life
So, wadda ya gunna do? Eh?

So that's your present, and a possible future
Think you're bloody smart, aye?
Well, the Old Testament and History
Is littered with the bones
Of fools like you, who are so arrogant
That they think their life is their own
And that God is merely philosophy.
When you are burning in hell
There will be nothing you can do.

What do you feel:
When your ranting pastor;

When your Rabbi or Imam;
When your Yogi or Bagwan;
When your Priest with wet fish handshake;
Or established protestant Dupe;
Speaks to you?

Parroting false interpretations from their Lizard Lips
The spittle they spray all over you and the congregation
Is coloured with the blood and pus of their covert hatred
But that is not to say in any way at all
That there aren't good men among these
Just that they are few and far between
For man has used since time began
Religion for gain and power
And when he does not like what he hears
He splits off and starts another sect
Just look at the trouble Jesus had
With the Pharisees and Sadducees
So wadda ya gunna do? Aye? Hmmm?

These blood soaked wolves in sheep's clothing
Because that is what they are, you know
Are sending you to the future
Heading you for a fall
But it's not their fault entirely
It's you that makes the choices
Just like Adam, given free will and all
No excuse or ignorance of wrong and right
You accept all the sugar coated shit
That you carry in your excess baggage.
There is someone who can guide you through
But truth is hard to take
You have to be very strong
So what can you do?

Let's get even more metaphorical now!
Back to these "Spiritual" leaders
And the rest who are on the same team.

Oh, they make you feel safe and secure
Leading you along to seeming abundant waters
Check out the fish floating upside down
Observe the trees planted in manmade rows
Amid the stumps of cedar, olive and oak
See barbed wire entanglements and bollards
Made ready to prevent escape, or to direct
You straight into the killing fields
Vehicles provided to bypass difficult places
But you find when you want to debus
You can't get off
There is nothing you can do
Look what happened to the Gypsy and the Jew,
The Irish, Khmer and Aboriginals too.
Act now or it will happen to you.

That is where the man in the pulpit;
That is where the man you voted for;
That is where the promise of the Market;
That is where the woman in the infomercial;
That is where the coat-hanger doctor;
That is where the car salesman;
And all the others, combined with your ignorance,
Pride, lust, envy, anger, hate, avarice and the rest
Wants to, or is, sending you to.
Yeah, up the bloody garden path.
Turn off the superhighway before it's too late
Or you never will have the choice
Of wondering what to do!

Come with me and others alike
Walk the black sheep trail, out of the land of death
Steep and rocky, with all obstacles imagined.
We have a guide to show us the way
Out into the wilderness, the desert you may say
If you don't like it, and are too scared to follow
The leader you can't see,
Well, go on your way, and let us go ours

Out here we have watchers and guards
You must have faith for them to help you,

They are waiting to walk beside us.
To help us when we stumble
Giving messages through others
Pointing out the abundance in a seeming desert
Food and clear waters
On tables laid out under the enemy's nose
No heavy baggage to carry
Only one bag needed
Everything else provided free along the way
If you are too frightened
Take a leap of faith
Then ask your guide to help you!
That's all you gotta do!
Take your noses out of those books
Tear your eyes away from that computer
Useless information only cluttering your mind
About as useless as a 100 watt bulb
Compared to a lightning bolt
Or a stadium floodlight
Compared to the power of the Sun
Man is losing his faith in God
Trying to do it without His help
The predictions of John the Divine
Are happening right here and now.
Get real, kneel down and bow.
No matter how much you claim
Is your doing and not luck or fate
It's one hundred percent the Father's Grace
That you go by, so be grateful, mate.

Get your nose out of that Book
Dripping with the blood of your Saints
Ironically the same Book they read
But not read with intellectual self will
The ONLY way to receive the Spirit

In order to be given the key
You covet so very much
To enable you to unlock the door
Put there by hate and prejudice
That imprisons your tiny mind
Is to ask. Yeah, ask Him.
If you ask who or wadda ya have to do, or who to pay
Read this over once more,
Pray, again and again – just pray
Or you might be on the wrong side of the Ledger.

When it comes to your Judgement Day.

THE COMING OF THE LAMB

THE LORD OF ALL: HOG HEAVEN!

THEY SAY HE MIGHT COME BACK RIDING A HARLEY DAVIDSON.

THE MAN

It's not the clothes that makes the man
No, it's the man that makes the clothes
If a man says it but doesn't do it
That makes him pretty much useless
He's got to do what he says
So he can say what he does.
They say the measure of a man's integrity
Is what he does when nobody is looking
By a man's fruits you shall know him
Not only by what he says
No matter how true he seems
A true man is worthy of another's trust.

The measure of a true mate
Is not what he's like when the good times roll
But how much he stands by you when the bad times come round
A man must be good, courageous and true
His mates must be too
A coward will only bring a good man down.

The Truth must be on a man's heart and the strength in his arms
And a man's fulfilment must be in his speech
A real man must be prepared to die for this
Men of this kind are Bobby Sands and William Wallace.

They meant what they said
Crazy Horse, Sitting Bull and Geronimo,
Martin Luther King, JFK and John Paul 2
The most perfect man of integrity is Jesus
He follows up on everything He says
He keeps His promises,
He is your best mate, stand by Him
Take courage and do what is right
He needs your help.

ABADDON

I WANT YOU TO DESTROY YOUR SANCTITY. I HATE SANCTITY. I WANT TO PERVERT JUSTICE - ACTUALLY ANYTHING. I WANT TO DESTROY THE DISTINCTION BETWEEN MALE AND FEMALE - ITS WORKING. IN ORDER TO DECIEVE THE YOUNG I WILL SEPERATE THEM FROM THEIR PARENTS INFLUENCE USING SOCIAL MEDIA AND TECHNOLOGY. I WILL SEXUALISE THE YOUNG USING THE LBGTQ COMUNNITY. I WANT YOU TO ABORT YOUR CHILDREN. I WANT YOU TO MAKE WAR. I WANT YOU TO MAKE CHRIST-IANITY OUTLAWED AND IRRELEVENT - BELIEVE ME I AM SUCCEEDING. IN PARTS OF THE WORLD. I WANT YOU TO BLUR THE DISTINCTION BETWEEN SHOW BUSINESS AND POLITICS. I WANT EDUCATORS TO ABOLISH FREE THINKING. I WANT TO TURN WISE OLD MEN TO RAPING CHILREN. I WANT MILLIONS TO STARVE. I WANT MANKIND TO THINK HE IS AUTONOMOUS. I WANT TO LAY YOUR SOUL TO WASTE. I WILL PROMOTE THE EXTREMES OF LEFT AND RIGHT UNTIL THERE IS NO DIFFERENCE. I WILL PROMOTE HATE WITHOUT REASON. I WILL PROMOTE THE IMAGE OF MOTHER AND CHILD AS THE ENEMY OF PROGRESS AND THE ENVIRONMENT. I WANT CHILDREN TO HATE AND DISHONOUR THEIR PARENTS. I WANT TO SET MEN AND WOMEN AGAINST EACHOTHER. I WANT TO BAN DISCIPLINE EXCEPT AS A FORM OF PERVERSION BECAUSE ITS ROOT WORD IS DISCIPLE. I WILL WHISPER SWEET NOTHINGS IN YOUR EARS. I WANT PEOPLE TO PURSUE GREED AND PERSONAL GAIN OVER THE COMMON GOOD. I WILL ENCOURAGE YOU TO PURSUE RIDICULOUS PURSUITS IN THE GUISE OF ENLIGHTENMENT. I WILL ALWAYS BE THERE WITH YOU IN YOUR SLAVERY TO YOUR ADDICTIONS. I WILL EXONERATE YOU FROM ANY GUILT BY MAKING YOU SAY "THE DEVIL MADE ME DO IT." I WILL ABANDON ALL MY FOLLOWERS AT THE HOUR OF DEATH AND LEAVE THEM FORLORN, ALONE AND IN ABJECT TERROR. I WILL INFLATE THE EGO'S OF MANY IN THEIR SUCCESS THEN TAKE EVERYTHING AWAY LEAVING THEM IN DESPAIR. I WILL TRANSFORM YOUR NORMAL MOODS INTO ABJECT MENTAL ILLNESS. I WILL BLUR YOUR SENSE OF RIGHT AND WRONG, THUS INFECTING TRUTH WITH RELATIVISM. IF YOU LISTEN TO MY SUGGESTIONS I CAN THEN OFFER ONE HUNDRED PERCENT CREDIT AND YOU CAN PAY THE INTEREST AT THE END OF YOUR LIFE. DO YOU GET IT YET? . I OFFER YOU MY PRODUCTS WHICH HAVE BEEN SUCCESSFUL IN CAUSING MAYHEM THROUGHOUT THE CENTURIES, YES THEY ARE PRIDE, LUST, INORDINATE DESIRE, ANGER, GLUTTONY, ENVY AND LAZINESS. IF MANKIND PURSUES THESE VICES AND HE IS PURSUING THEM HARD WITH A PASSION -, THE END RESULT WILL BE MORE WAR, FAMINE AND PLAGUE, JUST WHAT I WANT! HELP ME OBLITERATE HOLINESS, DECENCY, COURAGE, PRAYER, LOVE AND CONTINENCE FROM THE HUMAN RACE ...

... AND YOU WILL BE MINE!

απατεών, ASMODEUS

If you want to follow me or even better become a disciple of mine, I will protect you. If you don't want to, refer to the previous page. You can find me in the Gospel. You can find me in the Blessed Sacrament. You can find me in other people. You can find me in creation. But most of all you can find me in your heart. Where I need your help you will find me in the face of the poor, marginalised, mentally ill, oppressed and even the rich and seemingly self confident.

Life at times seems hard and unfair, but if you persevere with me you will achieve victory, especially in spiritual warfare. I will, if you ask me, take away your anger, fear and anxiety, not to mention depression and replace it with steadfast courage.

I am the Alpha and the Omega, the first and the last and no-one can come to the Father except through me. Knock and the door will be opened to you. No man can close it except me. If you want peace amidst the turmoil of the world, just ask it of me and I will give it to you.

HOSANNA!

THE WALK

Keep on walking and don't look back
When the vultures come down from the trees
There's no point in hanging around
It's all done and dusted, no point in crying
The milk has been spilt, nothing more can be done
Your battle may be lost, it may be won
Just keep walking.

You will burn bridges and make enemies
Hurt people and break hearts
Maybe you'll forgive and be forgiven
And then again, maybe not
It's all up to you and also to them
You've just got to keep going
Just keep walking.

Your body might get hurt and your mind broken
You will heal but there will be scars
And you will find out nobody cares
Because everybody's got their own walk
And that it's tough enough going
Without having to carry someone else
Just keep walking.

Keep going and carry your load
If it gets too heavy ditch the crap
In the walk of life it's best to travel light
And remember everyone lets you down
There are only two friends you can rely on
And they are Jesus and you
Just keep walking.

Walk the walk of LIFE
Not death.

For Daniel Sean Tohill

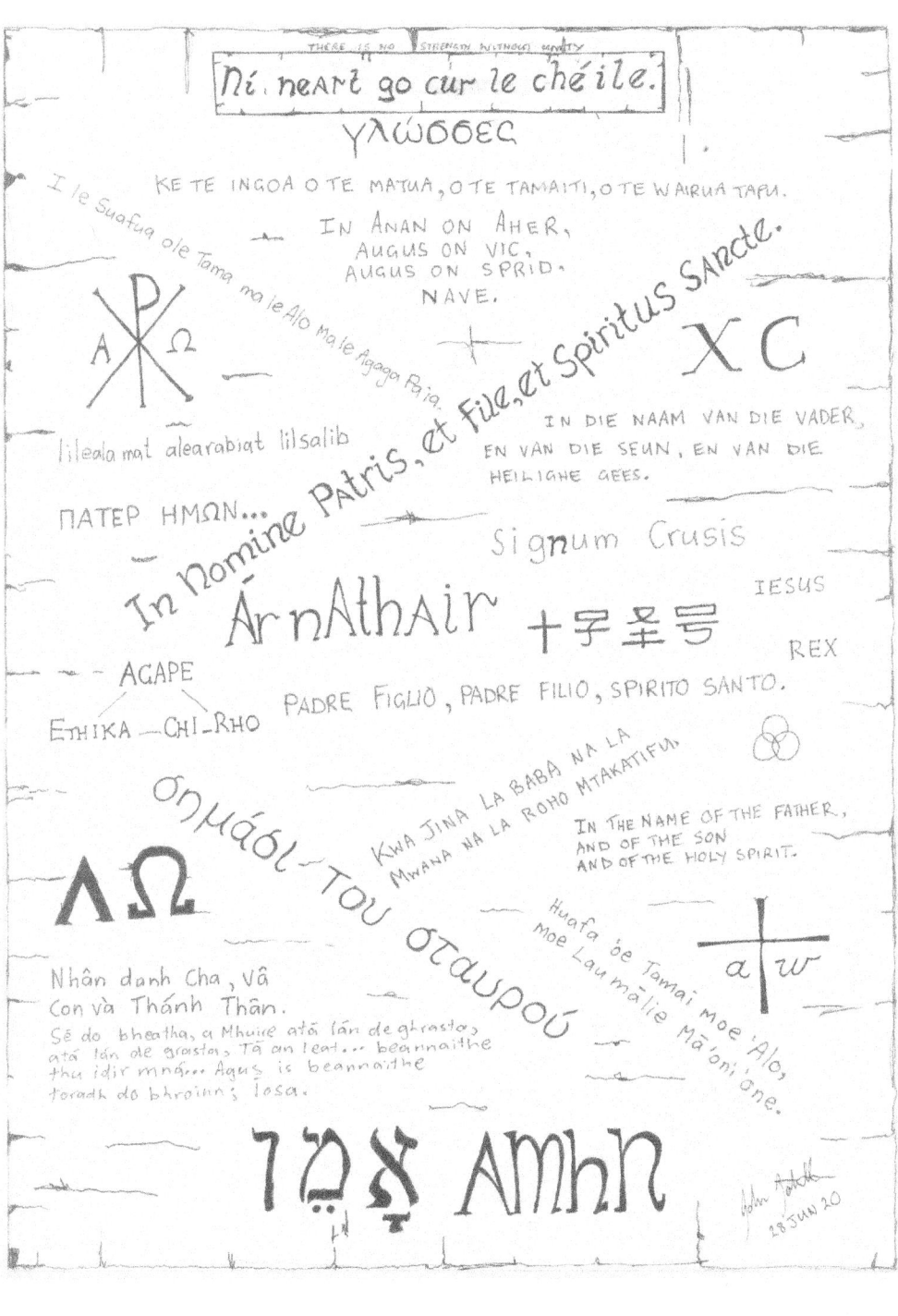

GOING HOME

The Catholic Church has got a flat tyre again,
She's been getting flatties for two thousand years.
They say she's the Kingdom of Heaven on earth,
The Church Militant, so the theologians reckon
Made up of the good, the bad, and the ugly,
Jesus won't have it any other way.

Saint Augustine said the Church is like a threshing floor,
Sorting the wheat from the chaff.
But if the wheats not on the threshing floor.
It's just wheat.
How can it be leavened into bread?

There are over a billion Catholics in the world,
So whatever you say about them will be true.
Adolf Hitler was a baptised Catholic
But then again, so was Mother Teresa.
Membership is from errant clergy and layity,
At one end of the scale,
To the greatest Saints and thinkers of all time.
Anti-popes, skulduggery and the Spanish Inquisition,
To the protection of family life, the unborn and the poor,
The whole range of humanity resides in Mother Church.

That's at any point in history.
She hasn't changed since Jesus gave Peter the keys.
She has seen kingdoms and empires come and go.
Always under attack from all sides, and from within.
Only getting bigger and stronger every day,
The only institution to survive intact since Christ.
You've got to wonder why, if you've got half a brain
Our Protestant brothers have been asking that for a while.
Maybe it's something to do with the Holy Spirit,
That Jesus promised for her guide
I'd certainly tell them that for free,
Quite a few find out and are received

Ironically, quite a few jump ship too.

It really doesn't matter in the end
It's not the clothes you wear that makes you clean
But rather whether you have had a shower
Jesus searches the heart
You will find Him there.
It's not only church attendance and Bible reading,
Though this is a good thing and essential.
No, it's not only that that Jesus wants
It's how you treat the least, lost and last
That's where it really counts.

And that's what the Church does best,
Right from the Pope and Cardinals,
With all the pomp and apparent ceremony
Yeah, right up to the most important part of the Church.
That's right – you and me.

Go forth, you are sent
It's the only way to come home.

THE PT INSTRUCTOR

Jesus is my "PT" instructor, he's tough
He's a bit like the one at Burnham of old
But Jesus knows me better
Though a PTI has a pretty good grasp
Of a man's fitness potential
And it's got nothing to do with size or shape
It's about heart, or "apple" as the shearers say
It's what a man does when the chips are down
When there's nothing left in the tank
How come it's the little guy carrying the machine gun?
It should be the big man, but it aint.
The fat kid who overtakes the jack rabbits
Who used to tease him at school
Yeah, the tortoise and the hare.

But back to Jesus, now he's my PTI
He's the leader of my parade
He teaches me in the way a sergeant does
That physical fitness is important for a man
It goes hand in hand with mental toughness
But most of all it helps with spiritual attainment
Don't listen to the false teachers
Christian Spirituality must be worked at
Sometimes it's bloody hard
You think you've reached the top of the hill
Then there's another one you've got to climb
But Jesus is always there doing it with you
He's like the infantry instructor
He wouldn't ask you to do
Anything He wouldn't do Himself
Remember, He died a horrible death on the cross.

Jesus teaches you real man's stuff
That's not very fashionable in this world
Like courage under fire in spiritual warfare
Honour in the face of cowardice

Compassion for the least, lost and last
The ability to go the extra mile
He teaches you to overcome and leads you to victory
Not over people, but the real enemy, Satan
He teaches you to discern the enemy's subtle lies,
Empty promises of prestige and power.
But most importantly, He teaches you to love,
To have faith, and hope.
The opposite of hate, distrust and despair.
In short, it's tough work being a Christian
But as the saying goes,
"When the going gets tough, the tough get going"
It's the only way to get to the top of the hill
So you can do the next one!

YOU PRAY FOR WHAT YOU WANT...
         ... I GIVE YOU WHAT YOU NEED.

THE RIGHT THING.

I get angry about stuff,
Because I forget who is really in control.
And I know when I stop to remember that,
Things will go ok in the end.
Because it's all about trust.

There is a reason for things happening
And it seems the hardest thing to do
In this messed up world
Is to do what's right
If only we all did.

His will here cannot be done
Without our helping hand
The hard part is discerning
When to do his work
And when to leave it to him.

We know the two commands He gives,
To love God with all our heart and soul,
And with all our strength and mind.
The other to love our neighbour as our self.
Why is it so hard?
If only we did the right thing.

In memory of Daniel Gerard Tohill
Born 29 February 1932 died 8 May 2004

יהוה ישוע

Χριστός

"I KNOW ALL ABOUT YOU:
HOW YOU ARE NEITHER
COLD NOR HOT. I WISH
YOU WERE ONE OR THE
OTHER. BUT SINCE YOU
ARE NEITHER, BUT ONLY
LUKEWARM, I WILL SPIT
YOU OUT OF MY MOUTH."
REV 13: 15-16

SACRATISSIMUM
COR IESU

ΠΑΤΕΡ ΗΜΩΝ
ΟΕΝ ΤΟΙΣ ΟΥΡΑΝΟΙΣ
ΑΠΑΣ ΘΗΤ ΩΤΟ ΟΝΟΜΑ ΣΟΥ,
ΕΓΘΕΤΩ Η ΒΑΣΙΛΕΙΑ ΣΟΥ,
ΓΕΝΗΘΗ ΤΩ ΤΟ ΘΕΛΗΜΑ ΣΟΥ,
ΩΣ ΕΝ ΟΥΡΑΝΩ,
ΚΑΙ ΕΠΙ ΤΗΣ ΓΗΣ
ΤΟΝ ΑΡΤΟΝ ΗΜΩΝ ΤΟΝ
ΕΠΙΟΥΣΙΟΝ ΔΟΣ ΗΜΙΝ ΣΗΜΕΡΟΝ.
ΚΑΙ ΑΦΕΣ ΗΜΙΝ ΤΑ
ΟΦΕΙΛΗΜΑΤΑ ΗΜΩΝ,
ΩΣ ΚΑΙ ΗΜΕΣ ΑΦΙΕΜΕΝ ΤΟΙΣ
ΟΦΕΙΛΗΜΑΤΑΙΣ ΗΜΩΝ;
ΚΑΙ ΜΗ ΕΙΣ ΕΝΕΓΚΗΣ
ΗΜΑΣ ΕΙΣ ΠΕΙΡΑΣΜΟΝ,
ΑΛΛΑ ΡΥΣΑΙ ΗΜΑΣ ΑΠΟ ΤΟΥ
ΠΟΝΗΡΟΥ
ΑΜΗΝ

So, if anyone declares himself for me in the presence of men, I will declare myself for him in the presence of my Father in heaven. But the one that disowns me in the presence of men, I will disown them in the presence of my Father in heaven.

Do not suppose I have come to bring peace to the earth: it is not peace I have come to bring, but a sword. For I have come to set a man against his father, a daughter against her mother, a daughter in law against her mother in law. A mans enemies will be those of his own household." MATT 10: 34-36

"And still, I tell you that it will not go as hard with the men in the land of Sodom on Judgement day as with you."
MATT 12:24

BE QUITE AT PEACE AS REGARDS THE EXISTANCE
OF DIVINE LOVE IN YOUR HEART, CAST ASIDE
ALL THAT FUTILE ANXIETY AND HAVE NO FEAR.

SAINT PADRE PIO

BROTHER

He looks out through your eyes.
He feels your joy and pain.
He answers your questions: all the whys.
He shows that from your anger, there's nothing to gain.
He tells you that He is, yes He is.
You pray for once you'll have a perfect day,
That evil will not have his sway.
But you know that in your heart,
That's not how it's meant to be,
It's been like that right from the start.
He's right there with you on your cross.
He knows what it's like: been there too.
He's there waking the mile alongside.
He'll carry the load with permission from you.
Sometimes no one else is there.
But if you pray, He will hear,
And He will take you by the hand.
Lead you to where the road will take you,
To His Promised Land.

FREE BIRD

Lynyrd Skynyrd wrote a song about him
Though with a 70's post hippie slant
Every man wants to be a free bird
Only a few achieve that aim.

Right from when he was a boy,
All a man wants to do is run free,
To "slay the dragon and hunt the lion",
To be strong, straight and true,
To soar with the eagles and dive the deep.

How does a man be free like a bird?
Freedom must be more than running away,
To go fishing, hunting or diving.
Some do that to survive, and they aren't free
Freedom must be more than drinking with your mates
Or having any woman you want
Some will tell you, that aint free.

Freedom must be more than climbing the corporate ladder,
Expense account, long hours and stress,
That is not free.
Freedom must be more than a retirement plan
Slaving your working life for something that disappears
That is not freedom either.

So what is?
For a start, I reckon you only have the right,
Or the gift, if you like, of one day
And you gotta make the most of it
Bank what you achieve
In that twenty four hours,
To help build on the next one –
If you get it.
And you never know,
Today might be your last.

Get up before the sun
Watch him come up.
Be an early bird,
Get the drop on the sleepy heads,
Catch that worm,
Get out there and do it.
Give it the best you've got.

Whether you're a street sweeper,
A gardener, a rubbish dude,
Or a nurse, doctor or lawyer.
Go hard, do it right and do it well.
Put your hard work in the bank,
It's worth more than money.

The dividends pay better
And you will be a free bird
So don't try to escape
Just do it where you are,
And do it real well.

So many people are imprisoned
While on their pursuit of freedom
They are lured by the empty promises,
They get sucked in and can't get out.
They buy now, and have to pay later.

That ain't freedom,
That's the living dead,
Old before their time,
Going nowhere,
The price they pay for nothing and emptiness
Is increasing.
And every day, they pay more and more.

There is an answer
But they have turned their backs on Him
Yeah, the Free Bird
The Bird they cannot change.

INTERPRETATION OF "THE LONG HAIRED FRIENDS OF JESUS"

The guys with the wings are four of the Archangels that stand before God.

From left Gabriel with the horn; Raphael with the mic. and Michael with the guitar. The other winged Angel is annamed because the Bible only names three of the seven Archangels.

The three unwinged Angels are War, Famine and Conquest from the Apocalypse, I ommitted plague.

I am in the bottom right corner wearing Sackcloth gathering inspiration for my next drawing. Note I had long hair too in 1998.

The late Keith Moon is making a geust appearance on drums.

Jesus, King of the Universe is on the top left of the picture with a bemused expression on his face is wearing a Crown of thorns in tribute to manic-depressives everywhere.

The moon is on the ware, a great time for this creative soul.

Behind Jesus is the Morning Star which I hope will one day rise in your mind.

Footnote :— Raphael doesn't play an instrument He is a doctor but being an Archangel he is in charge of all the choirs.

John Mahshh
9 DEC 21

CONVERSION

Repentance to me is cleaning up, not cleaning out.
Changing my ways, not changing who God created.
Fixing what is broken, leaving what isn't.
Healing what is wounded, not what is healthy.
Renewing myself, not replacing what God designed.
Picking myself up, not putting myself down.
Being humbled by God, not humiliated by Satan.
Changing from being shameful, to being worthy of merit.

I say it is me that does this, but only partly.
I cannot do a thing without outside help.
Nobody can, that help comes from God.
Through the power of the Holy Spirit
And by the example of other converted people.
But ultimately I choose which path to follow.
And I can easily take a wrong turn.
Ending up worse than I was before.

I know I have to pray constantly.
Having total trust in Jesus, my King.
But how do I know I'm hearing His voice?
And not just talking to myself.
Jesus said, "by their fruits you shall know them."
Am I producing good fruit?
Or am I a branch needing to be pruned?
That's the point, we all need regular pruning.

THE MEANING OF LIFE
(Dog's Bums)

The meaning of life is you
Your birth was not an accident
Nor was mine.

You were put here for a purpose
And not someone else's
Nobody can walk your walk.

You are born
You live
You die.

Why?

Why are there great mountains
That were formed
Millions of years ago?

Why is the extinction of an insect
The cause of the downfall
Of a great forest?

Why does a dog piss on a lamp post
Then see another dog
And sniff his bum?

Why do people congregate
And form a worthless creed
Then hate people with another?

Why am I writing this?
Only to give myself question marks
And no answers.

But hang on

Maybe there is an answer
The one that eludes a lot of people.

Because of paedophile priests
The Spanish Inquisition
And Feminist Nuns

Yes, and the rest
Pomp and pageantry
And TV preachers

They have barred us
From the answer
Yes, the Truth

What is the Truth?
Who is the Truth?
Who is He?

This guy must be awesome
He created bum sniffing dogs
And great mountain ranges

Why?

I don't know
I'm just living
Yeah, getting by.

They say this guy is called Jesus
By the way
The King of the Universe.

Why wouldn't you like Him?
I do
Some people hate Him.

He's my best mate

How the hell can you have a best mate
That created mountains and bum sniffing dogs?

He does more than that
He gives meaning
To this existence of ours.

Let's ditch the bum sniffing dogs
And bunches of rocks
And get down to it.

You are the meaning of life
You underwent the miracle of birth
You are on a unique journey.

Your life has meaning
It has a purpose
You are part of a big picture.

You are not a random collection of molecules
    That have come together by chance
On an aimless meander.

That's bloody depressing
Darwin can take a run and jump
Jesus is where it's at for me.

Get real
And with honest eyes
Have a look around you

Things aren't quite right
As we all know
Can we save the World?

Hitler tried
Along with Stalin and the rest
Failed ideologies causing only death.

Jesus gives life
He gives life to the full
To those who love Him

But that's only half the equation
We must love one another
Even the least, lost and last.

How can you love a Hyena,
A Rat or a Stoat?
Jesus created them.

"Hyena" and "Rat" people
"Stoats" among us
Jesus created them too

Yes, we are good and bad fish alike
To be collected in a big drag net
To be sorted by Jesus at the end of time.

Do you want to be a bad fish
To be discarded at the end of time?
I suppose it's up to you.

Jesus achieved our redemption on the cross
All we have to do is co-operate with Him
He will save us

Even the convicted rapist, and the murderer
Even the thieving TV preacher
If they repent

Maybe even you and me
That's my next question,
Are there rats in Heaven?

THE CIRCLE OF LIFE?
MODERN THINKERS and the INDIAN

"Man has poor understanding of Life.
He mistakes Knowledge for Wisdom.
He tries to unveil the holy secrets of our Father, the Great Spirit.
He attempts to impose his laws and ways on Mother Earth.
Even though he himself is part of Nature, he chooses to disregard and ignore it for the sake of his own immediate gain.
But the Laws of Nature are stronger than those of mankind.
Man must awake at last and learn to understand how little time there remains before he will become the cause of his own downfall.
And he has so much to learn; TO LEARN TO SEE WITH THE HEART.

He must learn to respect Mother Earth – she who has given life to everything: to our brothers and sisters, the animals and plants, to the rivers and lakes, the oceans and the winds.
He must realise the Earth does not belong to him but that he has to care for and maintain the delicate balance of Nature for the sake of the well-being of our children and of all future generations.
It is the duty of Man to preserve the Earth and the Creation of the Great Spirit, Mankind being but a grain of sand in the Holy Circle which encloses all Life".

White Cloud.

"Well, gentle men and women; you've just heard White Cloud's views on Life. I would like to hear yours. I'll throw open the forum starting with you, Mr Swaggart".

"Well, thank ya Sean. Ah would like to take issue with White Cloud's talk of the "circle of life". Everybody that's bin saved knows that bah readin' the babble for oneself, life began at Genesis Chapter One and finishes very soon at Revelation Chapter twenty three. THA AH END UV THA WORLD, Sean, mark mah words – by the way, it's all in mah updated CDs and DVDs, just ba ringin' free phone 1800 777 777 ya can purchase not only them but my books and classic babble tracts, ah-huh! Anyway, where was I? Oh yeah, who was the-us White Cloud anyways? Had he accepted Jeezus Chraist as his personal saiveeur? He'd be in the fars uv heeul if he don't. All that nature stuff don't sound vary Chrustian to me, Sean.

And ya caint read the good book with yer heart, ya gotsta use yer eye an yer brain an with the help uv the Wholly Ghost ya kin enterperate it fer yerself. Ya just gots ta know thee Gareek an tha Haybrew – it takes a few years bit ya git thar. An everybody knows there aint no "Great Spirit" that's just Papist propaganda promoted ba tha Ainti Chraist. Ah believe in Jeehova – Paraise the Lord – Amen!"

"Well, thanks for that, Jimmy. At this point I'd like to introduce Tama Iti, a notable member of Aotearoa's Tuhoe Iwi. Tama, what are your comments regarding White Cloud's statements?"

"Didn't go far enough, Sean. He didn't mention Tino Rangatira tanga at all, we can't go with that at all aye bro."

"That was very short and to the point for a warrior of such eloquence as you, Tama. Thank you.

Now I'd like to introduce the newly elected co-leader of the Green Party, Materia Turei. What are your thoughts, Materia?"

"Lots of sexist, outdated, patriarchal talk of respecting the "motherhood" of the earth, Sean. Why can't the Great Spirit be a Mother? Everything he says has a male bias. What about co-leadership? And yes man definitely has a poor understanding of things. What about women?

These Indian women obviously weren't allowed an education. Its just not inclusive enough Sean – and what about Gays? This statement needs to be brought into the 21st century. What if Mother Earth doesn't want to give life to everything? Surely it's her choice! The deep seated sexist issues evident in what he said just aren't in line with Green Party policy, Sean."

"Thank you very much for your thoughts, Materia. It's obvious from what you shared; New Zealand universities are real giants of Intellectualism. You are a fine example".

"Why ... thank you, Sean".

"I would now like to introduce a well-known Nelson Scientist and self-proclaimed population control expert, Professor Richard Cranium. Richard, what's your take on White Cloud's very popular treatise on the State of Mankind?"

"Well, I have – no due respect for this rubbish; he has no peer review – I have utter contempt for White Cloud's erroneous statements. He sounds very Creationist for a start and he talks about children! I mean to say, Ethnics – Bah! All they want to do is breed. It's quite obvious natural selection was at work in his day. I mean the white Anglo Saxons came in and wiped out his whole way of life –if that's not proof of Darwin's theory, I don't know what is.

His statements are simply not good science, pure and simple.

Now, look at me living in comfort in my tidy suburb, rattling around in my comfy retirement investment full of antiques obtained from distant lands – including Indian artefacts. I've got everything, Sean.

It's very quiet around here too. We don't have to put up with noisy children and we don't see that horrible sight of pregnant women pushing prams either. I can walk down to the local park and not see anybody under 40 – it's great Sean. You wouldn't get that in the world White Cloud dreamed of".

"Thanks, Richard. Now I'd like to introduce my final guest, Father Giuseppe O'Flaherty of OPUS DEI. What do you reckon, Father?"

Well, Sean, to use the vernacular, this statement is a cracker! Top stuff, sound if ya like. I passed it on to a couple of me mates at the Congregation of the Doctrine of the Faith – you, know, the Inquisition – and they gave it due consideration. They reckoned it was top stuff too. They couldn't believe it, Sean." All that White Cloud said can be found in Sacred Scripture AND the Catechism", they said. Amazing, considering he had probably never even read the Bible. "Couldn't take anything away from it", they said."

"Do you think Mankind might be going round in circles, Father?"

"Well, some of us are, Sean".

"Repeating the same old mistakes, you mean?"

"Well, yes. God gave us Mother Nature, Sean. If we mess with Mother Nature she won't feed us. The same as if you dishonoured your own Mother – if she is anything like my dear old Ma, she won't feed you either. Do you follow, Sean?"

"Yes, I do Father. That's food for thought. Well, thank you to all my guests on the panel. Next week we will discuss Einstein's Theory of Relativity."

HAVE JESUS WILL TRAVEL

I always feel that my position is tenuous
And that disaster is imminent
There's too much shit to worry about that doesn't matter
Like the fact there are mice in the pantry
The straw keeps getting loaded on the camel's back
Right at the time I just don't need it
I don't want it no more.

Then there are the times I have to explain my actions
Even though things usually pan out
Seems I'm never given the benefit of the doubt
Though I've been proven by what I've done
Many times before and I will again.
Sick of being a reflection of other's fears
I don't want it no more.

The danger with middle age, as I see it
Is growing man tits and acting like an old woman
A mature man shouldn't be like that
So what's the million dollar answer?
I certainly can't answer that vexing question
But being a man might be what's required
This is something I'd want.

For a start, I'd refuse to meet deadlines
And I'd knock over danger signs and piss on them
I would go to bed early and get up with the birds
I would rid myself of life's excess baggage
And carry a bag containing only what I need
That's something I'd want.

It is said the Sioux warrior, Crazy Horse
Had the power to dream himself into the real world
And to leave the illusion behind
That's the point, most people live in an illusion
The real world is too frightening

But for a man, the real world is where it's at
What Crazy Horse had is what I'd want.

Freedom is what Crazy Horse fought for
Not to mention the safety of women and children
He took a chance, challenged the mighty U.S. cavalry
And on the day he fought Custer and beat him
Though they got Crazy Horse in the end
But no one could have accused him of cowardice
That's the kind of man I'd like to be.

What is it like for Western men today?
We're not even called men now, merely males!
The only ones that get any kind of cred these days
Are Gays, Metrosexuals and Snags
I would say most of them are actually boys
Where are all the real men?
That's what I'd like to know

What does it take to be a man?
Where the hell are they all?
How do you become one?
What is the rite of passage?
Is there any these days?
I've had to ask Jesus in desperation.

Jesus is the ultimate Man
This is something I do know
He was like Crazy Horse, he didn't back down
He was the ultimate Spiritual Warrior
And He won – for all time
I would like to be in His motley band

What do men in Jesus' motley band look like?
Bravery and loyalty would be two characteristics
He could be a supermarket trolley guy
Or a lawyer, politician or All Black
Though I'd probably bet on the supermarket dude
How can you tell?

Jesus and His Disciples always travelled light
He has plenty of disciples today, men and women
But I'm talking about men here
They are mostly "tax collectors" and sinners
Fishermen, shearers and the like
He eats and drinks with them too
The Bible tells me that.

Back in early A.D. the Disciples took a chance
They followed Jesus where ever He went
Not a few women did too including His Mother
They saw an authentic free-thinking Man
Who always told the Truth no matter what
In fact, He is the ultimate Truth – the Son of God
How do I follow Jesus?

To be a disciple I have to be taught
The root word of discipline is disciple
That means training of a kind not popular today
It produces self-control, orderliness and obedience
Especially concerning Spiritual matters
It prepares a man for Spiritual battle
One we ALL have to fight.

The enemy we have to fight is Satan
Jesus has already beaten him
But now it's our turn, with Jesus help
And if you think we have already won
Just look around at the evil in the world today
Many have tried to fight Satan on their own
They just leave a big mess.

How do I travel with Jesus?
By praying with Him and trusting Him to show me the Way
But I have to travel with Him on the right path
And that path is the way I live.

MARAN - ATHA

He gives you that feeling
Like the roar of a shyhawk jet, just above your head
Like the sound of a chopper coming over a ridge
Like firing an assault rifle on full auto three hundred rounds to go
Like riding your Harley down the centre line at a hundred and sixty K's.
Like the sound of thunder above your head in a tropical cyclone
Like visiting your plot right under the cops noses
Like when you hold up your baby son for the very first time
Like only a good woman can give to a man
Like a visit from an old mate at your lowest time
Like escaping a beating relatively unscathed.

He gives some this feeling
The feeling of His power
The power of His feeling for mankind
To some if feels good
Some are filled with fear
But one things for sure
He tells me He's very near
And I am very glad
    His power transcends space and time
He lies out beyond the universe
Our existence is His recreation
    We should be thankful
That one day He will come to us
And we will feel that way all the time!

SEAN O'TUATHAIL

SUPERMARKET BAGS

The Persians must have thought the world was going to end,
When Alexander the Great and his army came through.
People must have thought the end was near,
When the Bubonic Plague swept through Europe, too.
The Mayans and Aztecs must have thought their time was up,
When the Spanish brought pillage, disease and slaughter.
At any point in history, somewhere, some time
The Prophets of Doom see disaster coming
Sometimes they are right, but it's never been the end
Last century it was nuclear holocaust and Y2K
Today it's climate change and over population
And, of course, there's the threat of total whiteout
From massive clouds of plastic supermarket bags.
Then there's the radio and TV preachers,
They've revised the date from century's turn
But Jesus is coming to destroy the world, they say,
To wreak vengeance on us unrighteous creatures
Some even say He is going to rapture the saved before the end.
Maybe, maybe not. Does it really matter?
One thing I believe, for sure,
And that is, the day I die
I will have reached the end of time
I will be in eternity and I'll go left or right
After being judged.
Maybe even on what I did with supermarket bags
About the world, though, I'm not worried.
I just pray – Glory be to the Father
And to the Son
And to the Holy Spirit,
As it was in the beginning
Is now and ever shall be
WORLD WITHOUT END
AMEN

OL' JOSHUA'S TREE

Come on honey come with me
Let's shake all the apples on ol' Joshua's tree
They are ripe and ready for a fall
You know you can have them all
Stranger step into the light
I never expected your love tonight.

Come on baby let's go with me
Give me some of that sweet release
I've travelled years marching all lands
Still got empty heart, holes in pockets and idle hands
But woman I do believe you are a sight
Never expected your love tonight.

Come on spunky let's go with me
If you find someone don't let them leave
Our Father has ordered from on high
We all gotta go forth and multiply
I do believe he got that right
I am grateful for your love tonight.

Come on darling let's go with me
Some think they own the light, have sole copyright
Create a shadow they have no right
Bad seed swept under condom carpet
Try to fill empty hole only making it deeper
Hateful and alone, in terror of the grim reaper
Life is kids and kids are lfe
So let's get it on tonight!

(A slight ripoff of Four men and a dog)

THE BOOK

What does the Holy Scripture say to you?
And does it matter today anyway,
In these "enlightened" modern times.
Why does a book that takes up to three years to read,
Have a message that is so fundamentally simple?
Whoops, I used the F word.
The Bible is full of many stories,
Of murder, theft, adultery, chicanery and betrayal.
The false teachers don't pick those ones out,
Because they are too close to the bone.
But these stories show the honest reader one thing,
And that is, man's condition has not changed.
Some dodgy things have been done in the Bible's name
And if you think it has a lot of words
Just imagine too, all the verbiage
Written in Its name over the centuries
Piled as high as The Tower of Babel
Now that's a misunderstanding.
To me its message is fundamentally clear
There goes the F word again
That the Bible is a handbook or tool for us
To carry on our journey
A map if you like
But we have to be taught how to use it.
We have the map but we still need to be shown the way
And how to enjoy the journey to the full
How to reach our final destination
And to ask the one that helped write this book
Who left a helper to interpret it for us
Someone gentle as a dove
He guides our Church for us
Who in turn interprets the Book
In order that we don't go off course
He is called The Holy Spirit
And he leads guides and shows the way
Because we ourselves have a tendency to stray.

PROFESSOR DICK SHINNERY'S MEANING PAGE
Sola Scriptura

By Scripture alone:
"Interpretation of the Bible should be up to the individual, guided by the Holy Spirit"
A few hundred years ago a Protestant gentleman, formerly an Augustinian Monk, came up with this brilliant idea.

Question One:
How do you know the Holy Spirit is guiding you?

Question Two:
How can you test it's the Holy Spirit and what if someone else's Holy Spirit differs from yours?

Question Three:
What happens if an idiot interprets the Bible for himself?

Question Four:
Does it follow that he gets an idiotic interpretation?

Question Five:
How can an idiot discern the inspiration of the Holy Spirit without help?

Question Six:
What if another idiot tries to help him?

Idiot: (noun) Person too deficient in mind to be capable of rational conduct.
(Pocket Oxford Dictionary)

Next time:
By Faith not Works.
Or maybe, an in-depth dissertation on re-inventing the wheel.

UISCE FE TALAMH

I am from out of the east
One of the four chief directions
Some call me Uisce – that is water
Water to put out your fire
I am the long reaching spear
The spear that some call destiny
Point forged from out of the Earth
Flying true through the Air
Speeding straight toward the west
Toward the setting sun.

Why do I do this? You ask
When most look the other way
Well, it's because I was born to
And there are lots about you
Who also walk against the prevailing winds
There are more and more every day
Answering to the calling dream
Awakened while still fast asleep.

We strive to separate from the illusion
In the process feeling the growing pains
Separating from a world swept up in delusion
The great outpouring of Spiritual waters
Has now begun to flow
Water from beyond the universe
    finding its way to us and maybe to you too
Into the deep inner space of our Souls.

The key to freedom was offered long ago
By the King of all Creation
The locked door is our hearts and minds
It is up to us to turn the lock
And open this door to freedom
Freedom and peace we crave so much
So if you see a light forming within

Behind self-inflicted veils of prejudice and sin
Don't abuse what you are being given
Acknowledge the bright new star
That is rising in your mind
Your life depends on it
Because it's the sign of a new dawn
A new day, blue skies and a new way.

VICTORY

How do you claim the victory Jesus, our Saviour won?
Do you read the Bible diligently?
In doing this, do you find fault in people you hate
Thereby exonerating yourself from your own guilt?
When you point the finger there's three pointing back
Is that victory?

Do you think victory is being "Spiritual"
And having an ambient stress-free life?
Do you think Transcendental Meditation
And relaxation music will do the trick?
Do you think cleansing your aura
And centering your chakra will make you feel better?
What about tarot cards, horoscopes,
White magic, and Celtic mysticism?
Will these give you power over people and the future?
Maybe Spiritualism, and talking to the dead?
Then there's the good old Psychic,
Are any of these victory?

What about money? How much do you need for victory?
Can you claim the victory Jesus won
With a comfortable retirement, and financial independence?
Climbing the corporate ladder
Or carving out a little fiefdom in your work place?
Does being on the Church Council
Or being a local body official or politician give you victory?

Does being an activist school teacher
And imparting your strange values on impressionable kids
Give you victory?
Is that the victory Jesus won?

Does being strong, fit and fast
Give the kind of victory we are talking of here?
Does being handsome or beautiful and having the gift of the gab
Bring victory?
Does having no laws and no limits
Bring people under the age of twenty, victory?
Does winning a military engagement
Thereby destroying infrastructure and displacing women and children
Bring victory?
Does "terminating" the unborn
And providing the old and infirm with an easy "exit"
Bring society victory?

Can any of these achieve the victory Jesus won? No.
What is the victory Jesus won?
It is victory over one of His so-called best mates who
Wanted to sell the ointment and give the money to the poor
And who betrayed Him to evil men with a kiss.
It is victory over evil
Evil is not a word or an action
It is a person.
He tells lies, makes empty promises
And he incites people all over the world, throughout history,
And with their witting or unwitting co-operation
To do stupid things that cause trouble for other people.
People who co-operate with evil, suffer the same fate
As Jesus' best mate
If they continue that behaviour without changing their ways.

In other words, these people die
Not the first death but the second death that comes after judgement
You don't want to go there
Since the first death could come at any time

Like when the boy racer crosses the centre line and he's coming at you
You have ten seconds
You are about to meet Jesus.
And you are about to find out
He is your Lord and King
The Power and the Glory
And you will find out if you have been his friend
You will find out why He has victory over death
Because the winner takes all
He takes His friends, He rescues them from death.

Who are these friends of Jesus?
I'd say Mother Teresa is probably one,
My Mum, of course.
No you can't name names
That's the job of Jesus and His Angels.
The Catholic Church has named not a few Saints
But she hasn't condemned anyone –
Not even Judas (aforementioned), Oliver Cromwell or even Martin Luther.
Will you go up or down?
I think it is up to you.
The only person who can send you to Hell is you
It's not what you say, it's what you do.
By your fruits Jesus shall know you.
Jesus loves us like His best friend or mate
He gives us a whole lifetime to realize that
But there comes a point when it's too late
The best time to become His friend
Is not some time in the future
When you've finished being naughty
But right now
And you will live life to the full
You will have victory
Over death.

WHO ARE YOU?

Are you the one that peddles a simplistic literal interpretation of the Bible in the guise of a big haired TV evangelist with a southern accent? Preaching covert hatred and setting one man against another.

Are you the one that peddles that New Age crap to the bored, spoiled and pampered who are too gutless to face the fact? Convoluting the old ways, diluting them, banishing them from the truth and repackaging them as enlightenment.

Are you the law maker with the secret agenda pulling the rug out from men and women struggling to raise families?

Are you the one that invented the silly cappuccino and latte' culture, your flunkies sitting there wearing Gucci, Dior and Klein? While down the street some homies are sniffing glue and some SKINS are having a revival meeting in the warehouse next door.

Are you the ethos of human rights, but the abdication of individual responsibility?

Are you the man that drinks from the Judas cup while telling your fair weather friends you possess the vintage wine?

Are you in the habit of trying to look at the big picture through the wrong end of a telescope?

Are you always vomiting up the truth because of your yellow appetite?

Are you always telling people you know the whereabouts of the Lamb's thorny crown?

And do you believe the doctor when he tells you that cats can fly and pigs can see the wind, but God can't be proved?

"...Then it will be their turn to ask, 'Lord when did we see you hungry or thirsty, a stranger or naked, sick or in prison, and did not come to your help?' Then he will answer, 'I tell you solemnly, in so far as you neglected to do this to one of the least of these, you neglected to do it to me'. And they will go away to eternal punishment, and the virtuous to eternal life." Matthew 25:44-46

"There was a lawyer who to disconcert him, stood up and said to him, 'Master, what must I do to inherit eternal life?' He said to him, 'What is written in the law? What do you read there.' He replied 'You must love the Lord your God with all your heart, with all your soul, all your strength and with all your mind and your neighbor as yourself.' 'You have answered right' said Jesus,

"Do this and life is yours." Luke 10: 25-28

Seán O'Tnathail
A Lifetime

YEHOSHUA

You start by thinking about this dude who split history in half and walked around Judea two thousand years ago wearing a white sheet and getting followed around by a bunch of misfits and fishermen.

He did, but I don't know about the white sheet, maybe that's the result of some later Italian artist's impression. You can't go fishing in a white sheet – you'd drown.

He healed the sick, the blind and the maimed, just with the touch of His hand.

Doctors today won't believe that, but He did.

What Jesus did mostly was to heal the Spirit – a word not found in medical dictionary's much today.

He spoke out against the hypocrites of His religion. They are still around today. People who are arrogant and who think they are a cut above the rest – people like you and me. And that's any hypocrite, not just the ones you encounter at Sunday Mass. People who "say" but don't "do".

In the three years of His public ministry, He had such an impact on the hypocrites that they had Him condemned to the most cruel death of those times.

He started a movement that is now well over two billion strong and growing rapidly. You wouldn't think so in countries like New Zealand, but we aren't the world.

How has He done this?

Why can't Christianity be stamped out? Why are people willing to die for their faith?

Kingdoms and Empires have come and gone but the Church has survived all of them.

A totalitarian, patriarchal institution? Maybe to an outsider who's got a beef with the Church. Divorce and abortion are the usual bones of contention. But the hunger for power is behind a lot of it. And perverts.

The only power the Church has is the Power of the Holy Spirit, which Jesus gave her.

How can you buy that? How can you make laws against it? How can you take it by force?

People complain about the Church's wealth, pomp and pageantry. But I suppose any institution that has been around for 2000 years would accumulate a bit of (mainly donated) wealth and a few traditions.

Back to Jesus. What did He do that is so important?

He destroyed death. He took the rap for us. He gave us a free pass to the biggest banquet and party in eternity. Everybody likes to be the special guest at a party – you are that guest!

What do you have to do?

Just be yourself for a start. And believe in Him while striving to keep His two simple commandments.

There's been so much written about these two commandments, enough to fill the hard drives of the biggest super computers.

How do you explain them to the "learned"? Simple people get them right off.

I don't think Heaven will populated with pompous, arrogant people telling others what to do while they take the best seats.

Do you do that?

I think Heaven will contain a lot of heroic old ladies, cripples, the maimed, the abused, the least, the lost and the last, people who never gave up, warriors and soldiers who protected women and children, people who loved – in their own way.

The list could go on....

Jesus offers peace – peace amidst the chaos and bedlam of daily life. In fact, He helps you sort out the mess you have made of your life. He forgives your trespasses, no matter what you have done, and gives you another go. And if you fall over again, He will pick you up.

Bad things *will* come your way, but Jesus will be there to help you overcome. He gives you nothing you can't handle, you just need to have Faith in Him.

Even if you don't believe, He is waiting at the door for you to open it and to let Him into your life.

The rain falls and the sun shines on everybody, but all good things come from God.

If you have Faith in Jesus and keep His commandments, the enemy of our salvation, the Devil, will not surprise you. When you recognise him he will run from you because he is a coward. All you have to do is command him to leave you, in Jesus Name.

Simple – just pray!!

If you don't know how to pray just get a copy of the Our Father (the Lord's Prayer). Memorise it and pray it in all situations, good or bad. The Lord will hear you, sometimes He will say "no", but He will help you in His own way and time.

As for me, I've discovered the best mate I've ever had.

And by the way, the two commandments are: "love God with all your heart, mind and soul" and the second is "Love your neighbour as yourself".

You can hang the Bible and all the rules and regulations and laws on that. In fact, if you keep those two commandments no Just Law can touch you.

But the rub is, how can you love someone if you think you are a piece of shit?

Back to Jesus and some serious prayer.

As I said, Jesus is your best mate, He walks alongside of you. He will teach you that if you hate someone, it's more than likely because you hate something in them that you see in yourself. This is a tough one.

He teaches you that you are capable of terrible evil. He teaches you to clean your act up. Not being "squeaky clean and helping old ladies across the street". Not being a "Mother Theresa".

Although there's nothing wrong in that.

It's not about giving up smoking or drinking, not getting traffic tickets or refraining from dancing. If I thought that was being a Christian I would have given up before I started. I'm not a follower of Oliver Cromwell, Brian Tamaki or John Knox.

You will find Jesus in the strangest of places and in the most unexpected people.

You might find Him in yourself.

God created you to be yourself.

Not some clone.

So just do it.

Where the rubber meets the road.

And get the drop on the "clones".

And ask your best mate for help.

THE PHARISEE AND THE PUBLICAN
Luke 18:9-14.

He spoke the following parable to some people who prided themselves on being virtuous and despised everyone else. Two men went up to the Temple to pray, one a Pharisee, the other a tax collector. The Pharisee stood there and said this prayer to himself, "I thank you, God, that I am not grasping, unjust, adulterous like the rest of mankind, and particularly that I am not like this tax collector here. I fast twice a week; I pay tithes on all I get." The tax collector stood some distance away, not daring to raise his eyes to heaven; but he beat his breast and said "God, be merciful to me, a sinner.:
  This man, I tell you, went home again at rights with God; the other did not. For everyone who exalts himself will be humbled, but the man who humbles himself will be exalted."

HE GIVES A MAN KINGSHIP

By his obedience unto death, Christ communicated to his disciples the gift of royal freedom, so that they might "by self-abnegation (self-denial) of a holy life, overcome the reign of sin in them-selves."
  "That man is rightly called a king who makes his own body an obedient subject and, by governing himself with suitable rigor, refuses to let his passions breed rebellion in his soul, for he exercises *a kind* of royal power over himself. And because he knows how to rule his own person as king, so too does he sit as its judge. He will not let himself be *imprisoned* by sin, or thrown headlong into wickedness."

Saint Ambrose
CCC908

JUSTIFICATION
(A Treatise on James)

The faith you have is defined by your works. How can you be "saved" if you despise your brother? Your faith is in itself a work, because you have to constantly work at it. You can't just read about it in your favourite Translation. You've got to get out there in the world and do it, whether in a Cathedral, at work, in a club or wherever the rubber meets the road.

Works is the other side of the coin. The driver of your works is Faith. You believe in Him and because of that he tests you and he meets you every day, in all the people you will encounter. The world is where you will find Jesus in this life – you trust him, can he trust you? If that person whoever he is, who encounters you, sees a bit of Jesus present, well maybe you've helped someone else find him. So just be yourself, warts and all. Pray and trust in him and the world will turn for you.

And me.

Sean O'Tuathail
26 April 2009

The Lord, who has taken away your sin and pardoned your faults, also *protects* you and keeps you from the wiles of your adversary the Devil, so that the enemy, who is accustomed to leading into sin, may not surprise you.

One who entrusts himself to God DOES NOT DREAD THE DEVIL. "If God is for us, who is against us?"

Saint Ambrose

SIRACH 2:1-11
(Eclesiasticus)

MY son, if you aspire to serve the Lord, prepare yourself for an ordeal.
Be sincere of heart, be steadfast, and do not be alarmed when disaster comes.
Cling to him and do not leave him, so that you may be honoured at the end of your days.
Whatever happens to you, accept it, and in the uncertainties of your humble state, be patient.
Since gold is tested in the fire, and chosen men in the furnace of humiliation.
Trust him and he will uphold you, follow a straight path and hope in him.
You who fear the Lord, wait for his mercy; do not turn aside in case you fall.
You who fear the Lord, *trust* him, and you will not be baulked of your reward.
You who fear the Lord, hope for good things, for everlasting happiness and mercy.
Look at generations of old and see: who ever trusted in the Lord and was put to shame?
Or whoever feared him steadfastly and was left forsaken?
Or whoever called out to him and was ignored?
For the Lord is compassionate and merciful, he forgives sins, and saves in days of distress.

THEOTOKOS

WHY DOES THIS IMAGE FILL SO MANY PEOPLE (PROTESTANTS / WOMEN / FEMINISTS) WITH HATRED?

IRISH STEW AND CAMPBELLS MUSHROOM SOUP™

If Jesus came back during the Christmas season
What would he find?
A third of the world suffering from war
Another third of the world oppressed
And a third of the world thinking they were ok
But under the hegemony of rich people
Who can never get enough.

They gave them Santa Claus to make them feel better
He gives them gifts
But they have to pay the rich people for them.
They get the third of the world that is oppressed
To make them on the cheap i.e. for two dollars a day
A smart phone produced for 50c costs the gift giver much more
The rich people take the difference.

If the oppressed start an uprising
Against the rich people
The rich people create a war
And get the third of the world suffering from war
To make their smart phones instead
Creating peace for them
Which everybody wants.

Meanwhile the okay third of the world get complacent
And let some oppressed and war refugees in.
They want Santa Claus gifts too
Some want to make war on the okay people
For what they have done to their third of the world
They use smart phones to organise terror
Trouble is, the rich people are hard to find
They don't have borders
And they keep their money in cyber banks that are not really anywhere.

This causes a major head fuck for terrorists

Who bomb and murder other oppressed people who may look a bit rich and decadent
But everybody now has smart phones, the war torn, the oppressed and the okay.
The rich people are getting richer
The okay, the oppressed and the war torn are all mixed up without borders.
The rich people all move to Switzerland
And put out a rumour they live in Israel.

Everybody makes war on Israel
But Israel has special smart phone jammers supplied by the USA
This causes massive confusion.
The well off people embrace peace and tolerance
This creates a vacuum
The oppressed and war torn fill it
The world is at war with itself – and it stops raining.

The Israelis start making irrigation equipment
In preparation for the coming famine
The rest of the world is now thirsty and starving due to lack of water
The Israelis have the answer
But the rich and the terrorists don't want a bar of it
Because it will bring about peace.

Jesus arrives to our world disguised as an irrigation salesman
Half of the world's people, half of every third, hate him.
The others are just thirsty, they follow Jesus.
Even Santa Claus wants to but half of his elves don't.
Things are coming to a head.
Jesus is leading the world to water but only half want to drink
The other half want to make it difficult for them to drink.

A rich bastard called Damien decides to make war on Jesus
Damien is the Anti-Christ
He forms a massive multinational conglomerate
Manufacturing dehydrated foods
He gobbles up the world's food production
All he needs is water
And Jesus and His followers have it.

Jesus and His people play a waiting game
They grow their own food
And share it in common
Because they have Israeli irrigation equipment
At a fair price
They prosper.

Financed by the rich people, Damien enslaves the masses of oppressed and war torn
To make more dehydrated foods.
He takes the whole western world under his yoke
He prospers, they don't
Only the rich can afford enough water
It costs three times as much as oil.
Damien makes a decree
Anybody with his mark on their forehead could buy water at a discount
As long as they meet his conditions, which are:
Public denouncing of Jesus and the Israelis
Conversion to a world religion whose head would be Santa Claus
The deification of Santa Claus
Sterilization after one child
All abortions would be regarded as a sacrifice to Santa Claus (this would make women eligible for a ten per cent water discount)
All citizens would be issued with smart phones equipped with two way cameras (for safety and security he assured them)
The west continued to suffer severe famine.

Meanwhile in the Middle East where Jesus is based
The deserts start blooming again, food is plenty
Everybody gets on; they just forgive all the time
Large families are the norm
Nobody has smart phones anymore
What for? They would say
Everybody forgot their religious differences
And they just followed Jesus, even the Israelis.

Some thought it was the new Heaven
Jesus warned it wasn't yet

The other half of the world hate us, He said.
Nobody really hated the "Santa Clausians" as they called them
They just didn't want them to bring
Their way of life to their part of the world.

The Santa Clausians, under Damien's rule, had:
Enforced abortion
Gay marriage and adoption
Legalised paedophilia
A 40% tax rate
Water rationing
Life imprisonment with hard labour for hate speech
Execution for denouncing Damien
The making of Santa Clausianism the state religion
State funded child care centres specialising in Santa Clausianism early education
Re-education camps for minor forms of dissent.
Damien built up a massive army called the "One World Defence Force"
He formed the Damien Guard
Recruited from promising students of the One World Education system
The OWDF and DG had the biggest water ration of the whole western world
Another of Damien's measures was the formation of the Climate Change Police
They were recruited from the Green Party which was the only legal group apart from the Santa Clausians at that time.
Everybody was encouraged to grow vegetables with recycled water
Dairy, beef, pig and sheep farming was to be phased out because of CO_2 emissions
All log fires were to be banned for the same reason.
Coal use was also banned except for state industries
In particular the arms industry which supplied the OWDF
This was to preserve peace and defend the state from Jesus and the evil Israelis.
The Climate Change Police had a mandate for the protection of the Gay, Lesbian, Transgender and paedophile communities from hate speech or any form of discrimination.

They also policed the one child policy as this was for the purpose of saving that part of the planet.
All elective surgery was rationed due to the amount of abortions being performed.

JUMP THIRTY YEARS
Hordes of traumatised Damienites where sneaking over to the Middle East where the Jesus people lived.
They were welcomed
The women had fled because they refused sterilization
There had been fighting in the border areas from time to time
But the Damienites were no match for the Jesus militia
Mainly because the Damienites were aged
Due to the fact there weren't many young people to recruit.

The main reasons for the border incursions was the scarce resource of water
Which the Jesus people had plenty of.
The Jesus militia said "if you lay down your arms you can have as much water as you want".
This was a very successful tactic.
The militia always won their battles for one simple reason;
Bravery and tactics which was inherited from the old Israeli army
Which in turn had inherited it from the likes of King David of old
Remember they were being led by the Son of David.

The Western World was now starting to look like Caligula's or Nero's Rome.
More than 40% of the population was by now Gay, Lesbian, Transgender or paedophile.
The latter had been identified as excellent early childhood education teachers.
Nobody had any restraint any more,
The recently formed Tolerance Police saw to that.
They were a particularly militant division of the Climate Change Police
With the authority to summarily execute homophobes on site.
CCTV was all pervasive, even installed in the people's bedrooms.

The word "pervert" was removed from the new Western World dictionary
And many other words were also taken out

Or redefined and given a more "modern" meaning.
The Bible was banned
A new One World Peaceful Living tome was published
And every household was required to have one
And CCTV assured people were seen to be reading it.

By official decree feminism was elevated
To the third legal Western World religion
They were allocated their own police force
With powers equivalent to the Tolerance Police.
They were particularly active in the child care centres
Ensuring that young males were educated properly.

Back to the Middle East
The Sahara was now on the retreat
Much of it had now been irrigated
Great swathes had now been colonised by wildebeest, lions and all animals in between
The lions didn't bother the people and their stock
Because they had plenty to eat.

Black Africa was now allied to the Middle East
And were following Jesus
You know – love God and love your neighbour
Even white South Africans joined in
Though South Africa ditched the rainbow nation thing
As it was now the Western World's flag.

Jesus said "You don't have to.
It's a sign of My Father's covenant with Noah".
They said it had been perverted
Jesus said "Fair enough".
Because of the irrigation techniques reclaiming land
Africa now had plenty of room for more wild animals and people.

There was a new immigration phenomenon
People flocked from Scotland, Ireland, New Zealand and yes, Australia.
The Kiwis said "Our country has been taken over by bloody vineyards, and industrial farming that employs cheap labour".

Jesus asked "Why?"
"Cos we forgot our heritage"
"What's that?" asked Jesus
"A forty hour working week and a fair suck of the sav".
"Same here", drawled an Aussie.
Jesus always gave you an answer by asking a question. He could almost be Buddhist.
Well, he is Lord of them too.
A Scot and an Irishman chimed in
"We've been oppressed by the fecking English for centuries".
"Why?" asked Jesus.
"Because we forgot our Gaelic heritage", replied the Mick.
"Because we accepted foreign religion", replied the Jock.
"You have your answer", Jesus replied.

The people of the Middle East and Africa, along with the hordes of immigrants, lived happily
They grew stuff, built up, created and lived happily together
Inter marriage was the norm, acceptance of other cultures was welcomed
Acceptance of the <u>Truth</u> in all religions was welcomed also.
Everybody loved Jesus
He was regarded as a brother and not a Big one.
People loved each other too.

Money wasn't used much
Except for necessary transactions
Banks only held it for somewhere to put it.
Barter was the norm i.e. half a wildebeest for a damn good barrel of Sudanese lager.
Kids were educated by parents, elder siblings and the wider community and in that order.
Things were going back to the Clan system common to many peoples,
Without the conflict.

The Israelis were giving away their irrigation knowledge shekel free.
This delighted and amazed the Palestinians and Arabs.
Jesus said that the Israeli irrigation technology
Would be superseded by what was happening

And that was that everybody was planting trees now
And selectively logging so the resulting forest would still attract rain.

People worshipped God in their own way
And they found Jesus' way easy so they followed Him.
Immigrants came from China, Tibet, Vietnam, Scotland, Wales, England, Russia, Serbia
Croatia, Iran, Iraq, Yemen, Finland
Sweden, Fiji, New Caledonia, Solomon Islands
Japan, USA, Mexico, Ireland and all over the world.
Things were looking up for Jesus' kingdom
Thy will be done on earth as it is in Heaven.
But not for everybody on earth yet.
Yet.

It was one week before Christmas that year.
The Santa Clausians were in a frenzy.
Gay Elves dressed in tight shorts were in the shopping malls
Enticing the few kids who were around
To come and sit on Santa Claus' knee
And beg for presents.
More and more Santa and his Elves were dressed in rainbow colours
Rather than red
They said it was more tolerant
Of everybody's cultures, beliefs and thought processes.
People bought now and paid later with a vengeance
From the rich people
With the hope of water concessions.

BREAD and the CIRCUS
The ingenious method of Western World control
Was the smart phone, the internet,
And dehydrated food
Even dehydrated McDonalds, BK, and KFC
The catch was that people needed water.
If you had an adequate water allocation
You had made it.

But to get an adequate water allocation
You had to follow Western World customs, laws and regulations
These were: (and this is not an exhaustive list)
Absolute and utter devotion to Christmas shopping
Absolute and utter devotion to Easter shopping
And Valentine's Day shopping
Boxing Day sales and days of commercial significance
Having shopping mall passes appropriate to water allocation
Internet shopping that was monitored
Any shopping at all
Attending shopping workshops funded by the state.
Shopping with a water allocation card which was based on the old Fly Buys card.

To be able to attain water concessions and therefore the ability to go shopping
The people had to work twenty four seven
People worked to keep Damien happy
Damien was never happy, He always wanted more
Things were always tight
So the people tightened their belts
And worked harder, longer and apparently smarter
This almost pleased Damien
But not enough.

He and the One World Government instituted a further set of sacrifices.
To be instituted immediately
For the betterment of the "State" and the people of course,
For the Collective benevolent "providers" in Switzerland.
Who were fighting Israel and Jesus
To protect the people
From homophobia, inequality and environmental degradation.

On top of abortion as a sacrifice to material wealth,
Freedom of speech was to be banned
As it was a practice of the evil people in the Middle East
People were to sacrifice their spare time
For total devotion to their Apps, Internet and Smart phones

In order to keep up with the latest specials,
Movies, porn and instruction from Damien's Government
Which was their Saviour.

People were to sacrifice their thinking
For the betterment of the Great Collective
Which was Damien
Nobody knew what Damien looked like
But they knew he was watching
They knew he was looking after them
Keeping them safe from the evil Middle Easteners.

Damien made a decree
He said he had intelligence
Gained from his drones and satellites
That the Middle Easteners were about to make war on them,
That they were terrorists.
Nobody in the Western World liked terrorists
Because they prevented them from shopping.
War was declared on terror.

Meanwhile in the Middle East
They had heard of coming developments
Everybody's eye was on Jesus
Who, of course, seemed to be everywhere.
Nobody was worried though.

Missiles were fired from OWDF aircraft carriers
At Cairo, Beirut, Tel Aviv and Jerusalem
In fact all North African and Middle Eastern cities
Destroying them utterly
But it didn't matter
Because nobody lived there anymore
Except on a small mountain in Israel
And the plain of Jezreel or Maggedo
Which the Western World forces overlooked.

Damien's forces over ran the Temple Mount

And flew in pre-fabricated shopping malls
Jesus' people weren't worried
In fact they didn't give a shit!
They had the King of the universe as their leader.

Damien incited his army to abuse Jesus
Jesus deigned to reply with a question as usual
"Who is your master?"
The Westeners were incensed and moved to anger.

Damien's forces attacked and destroyed all the Middle Eastern shopping malls.
Nobody died because nobody was there.
Middle Easteners didn't go shopping any more.
Damien's real reason for invading the Holy Land was to secure
What he thought was a good water supply.

Jesus commanded it to not rain in the Santa Clausian held territory
All the rivers and reservoirs dried up,
Helped by the Israeli/Arab combined irrigation maintenance force
They knew where to turn the water off
There were soon water shortages in Santa Clausian held territory.
The Santa Clausian toilets couldn't flush due to lack of water.
Soon all the drains blocked
And the OWDF personnel started getting the shits.

The Middle Eastern army formed up on the Plain of Maggedo
The Scots and Irish divisions of the Middle Eastern army taunted the Santa Clausians.
They were good at that. Jesus thought it was amusing.
The Santa Clausian infantry were ordered to fight with no trousers
So it didn't matter if they had the shits.
The Santa Clausian supreme commander exhorted them to fight to the last man.
He recalled the Welsh bowman at the Battle of Agincourt
This didn't go down well with the Franco Santa Clausians though.
The Santa Clausians charged in a shower of shit
The Scots and Irish yelled out " Pooooo ya stinky feckers"

The rest of the Middle Eastern army broke up laughing
The Santa Clausians fled the field highly embarrassed.
The first battle of Armageddon was won by the Middle Easteners without a shot being fired. Nobody was killed. The Santa Clausians were outwitted by Jesus and His army.
Funny that.

The Middle Easteners checked out what the Santa Clausians had left behind on the field.
They found dehydrated mung beans and tofu stew in the ration packs
Plus low fat powdered milk and chocolate, SPF30 sunscreen, Condoms,
Water bottles containing Red Bull ™ and V ™
Rolls of toilet paper, Ancient 1990s Gulf War ammunition
Copies of Queen's Greatest Hits lyrics
Copies of Damien's speech urging "tolerance and care for the environment"

The Scots and Irish yelled at the Santa Clausians
"Don't worry darlings, ye can push it all back up tonight!"
Jesus rebuked them; "some of the people you are talking about might want to come over to us so they need to be treated with the same dignity as anybody else", he scolded.
"Right you are, Boss", the Scots and Irish contingent yelled
Treating Jesus with that same Celtic irreverence they had for everybody.

The OWDF made a counter attack air strike that night
They hit mostly their own lines. The missiles that hit the Middle Eastern lines were duds
The Cambodian Bomb Disposal Unit was sent in to defuse them
OWDF pilots were trained in the USA – so there you go
The OWDF subsequently withdrew to their own territory due to health problems.

All the Middle Eastern cities except Jerusalem were rebuilt
It was decided to accommodate the expected influx of defectors from the Western World in these cities.
Shopping centres were not rebuilt.

Life was getting more oppressive in the Western World. The trickle of defectors turned to a flood. They were expected. They were welcomed
They told horror stories of life under Damien and the rich people.
Instant train trips to the Bergen-Belsen hospital complex for second pregnancy mothers
Hard labour at Auschwitz re-education camps for suspicion of homophobia
Thinking classes for infants at child care centres based on feminist – environmental theory
Compulsory 24/7 shift work for non-party members
The total outlawing of any forms of alcohol.
Legalisation of cannabis
The extension of District Council powers to include control of individual household CO_2 emissions, composting household wastes and collection of whale saving contributions.
Every aspect of life had a regulation pursuant to a sub clause
It was in the sub clause that Damien had the power and control.
Except for the rich people
They weren't under control of any sub clauses
They had control from Switzerland
Damien was their puppet
He did their bidding ...

... Which was to control the world's food distribution
But it wasn't working
People didn't like dehydrated food much
Especially since Jesus and His people had the water
Which is why people were sneaking over to the Middle East
On top of all that, the Councils installed eftpos at all household water meters
User pays.

Left becoming right and right becoming wrong
It was too late for the Western World
A civilisation living in fear:
– Of homophobic Middle East
– Of global warming

- Of not having enough water
- Of Council officials
- Of Terrorists from the Middle East (though in reality there were none)
- Of getting pregnant
- Of missing bargains at the many sales
- Of hearing the name of Jesus which was now totally banned in all forms of media.

Damien exhorted in all his addresses that the Middle East was the true enemy of civilisation
And that the state had a plan. Another strike against them
But something happened in the meantime
Over the whole Western World it rained for forty days and forty nights
There were massive floods. The people didn't know whether to rejoice or panic
They looked to Damien for leadership
Damien said this was the time to attack the Middle East
While they weren't expecting it.
THE OWDF tried bombing the Middle Eastern cities again
To no avail
Because the Middle East had Kingdom air defence missiles
Descendants of the old Patriot missiles.
They didn't miss
The OWDF invaded Israel again
They grouped at the Maggedo Plain
The Middle Eastern forces met them there
Each side waited.

The Middle East had a secret weapon
Cans of Irish stew and Campbell's™ creamy mushroom soup
They used artillery to fire these at the enemy in cluster fashion
The OWDF were sick of dehydrated food
So they ate the millions of cans of soup and stew fired at them
But you needed a strong stomach to digest the stuff
The OWDF soldiers had weakened digestive systems
From years of eating dehydrated vegan food
They got the shits again. And couldn't fight.
The Scots and Irish division taunted them

This was too much
They surrendered and lay down their arms.
The final Battle of Maggedo was over.

Peace. Maybe
The Western World flora and fauna sprang into life after the floods
People grew their own food and water was plentiful
Damien was losing his grip on power
The rich in Switzerland were worried
What could be done?

The value of the Euro dollar plummeted
The shopping malls and banks went broke
All the money went back to Switzerland
The Western people just grew more food for themselves
The rich people didn't know how to control this
Damien went into hiding.

The local Councils took over
They granted themselves sweeping powers as usual
But they were easily outwitted
By the growing Jesus – friendly underground
Who had been secretly evangelised
By Jesuits sent by the beleaguered Vatican
Who had survived years of sanctions and persecution
Imposed by the Santa Clausians.
The Council officials were pre-occupied
With writing reports, lengthy policy documents and papers
And they seldom got out of their hybrid Suzuki cars
Their life was the PC and bits of paper
Containing meaningless verbiage
So basically the Councils were in their own world
A world far apart from Western Worldians
Who had now rejected Santa Claus
And didn't go shopping any more.
They now looked to the Middle East for leadership
And found it.
From Jesus and the former Western World refugees

Jesus said "from the hands of the liberated you will find liberation".

But the Western World was not liberated yet
They still had oppressive laws
They still had Bergen – Belsen and Auschwitz
And rampant out of control Academics
Who were much like Council officials
By now devoid of any relevant meaning
And who had nowhere to shop.

The Academics and Council officials turned on each other
Vying for power
Both groups tended to drive Suzuki hybrids
Both used the tactic of car bombing
Suzuki hybrids packed with explosives driven at high speed
Into Council buildings and university campuses blowing them up
Everybody now lived in fear of speeding Suzukis
Driven by crazed Academics and Council officials.

The population avoided places of learning
And Council buildings
For their own safety
The Council officials and Academics killed themselves off
Much to the relief of everybody in the Western World
Who were sick of having their lives tinkered with and regulated
There didn't seem much point in sociologists or any other "ologist" for
    that matter
In the newly emerging Western society
The populace didn't need them
They had Jesus to look to for wisdom.
The Western World gradually integrated with the Middle East
People who had offended Jesus were offered forgiveness
If they were sorry
The forgiven were happy to be free
Those people who weren't sorry left Jesus' kingdom
Never to return
A little boy asked Jesus were they went
Jesus just said "to a place of their own choosing"

The boy thought about what Jesus said
He said "I'll stick with you, Brother"
Jesus said "Go and play and don't think too much"
The little boy laughed.

The Auschwitz and Bergen-Belsen complexes were utterly destroyed
By Irish explosives experts
And trees were planted in their place
Nobody went there
The wild animals took over
Mother Nature gradually cleansed these places
Of the offences to Her

Jerusalem was rebuilt
A great hospital was constructed there
Many people went there for Jesus' healing
Especially the abused children
And women who had been affected by abortion
Everybody was healed
People who suffered envy, hate, lust, anger and the rest
Above all people were healed from fear.

Talks were held with the Dalai Lama
The Far East joined the Middle East and Western world
The world was now united under Jesus
Except for the people who refused forgiveness
And who refused to believe in Jesus
They died eventually.

Then something happened
It was universal
Ancestors of all people came back to life
Those who were forgiven
There were a lot of surprises!
There was another phenomenon
Nobody died!
People just lived in harmony
And had a good time doing it

Everybody could claim to have eaten with Jesus
At His Banquet
Death was no longer for the people of Jesus

Victory!
Jesus said "Victory over yourselves"

PS – Author hopes he has not offended people who like eating tinned Irish Stew and Campbell's Mushroom Soup

© John Tohill 2022

PSALM 23

The Lord is my shepherd;
I shall not want.
He makes me lie down in green pastures,
He leads me beside still waters,
He restores my soul.
He leads me in paths of righteousness
                         for his names sake
Even though I walk through the valley of
                the shadow of death;
I will fear no evil.
For you are with me; your rod and staff
                               comfort me.
You prepare a table before me in the
                Presence of my enemies;
You anoint my head with oil; my cup overflows.
Surely goodness and mercy shall follow me
                all the days of my Life,
and I shall dwell in the house of the Lord,
Forever.

THE ECONOMY OF SALVATION

Go brother, you are sent.
Fear nothing and love me.
Live your life to the full.
But don't hurt anyone.
If you fall over, pick yourself up.
If you can't, I will help you.
Be my hands and be my feet.
Pray always and speak the truth.
Your road will be hard but so was mine.
I am always with you.
Trust in me and your joy will be complete.

Appendix

Appendix

COMMUNITY

Be at peace among yourselves. And this is what we ask you to do, brothers; warn the idlers, give courage to those who are apprehensive, care for the weak and be patient with everyone. Make sure that people do not try to take revenge; you must all think of what is best for each other and for the community. Be happy at all times; pray constantly; and for all things give thanks to God because this is what God expects you to do in Christ Jesus.

Never try to suppress the [Holy] Spirit, or treat the gift of prophecy with contempt; think before you do anything – hold on to what is good, and avoid every form of evil.

1 Thessalonians 5: 12 – 22

DON'T TURN AWAY

If, after we have been given knowledge of the *truth*, we should *deliberately* commit any sins, then there is no longer any Sacrifice for them. There will be left only the dreadful prospect of judgement and of the raging fire that is to burn rebels. Anyone who disregards the Law of Moses is ruthlessly put to death on the word of two witnesses or three. AND YOU MAY BE SURE THAT ANYONE WHO TRAMPLES ON THE SON OF GOD (my emphasis), and who treats the blood of the covenant which sanctified him as if it were not holy, and who insults the Spirit of grace, will be condemned to a far severer punishment... We are all aware who it was that said: Vengeance is mine; I will repay. And again: The Lord will judge his people. It is a dreadful thing to fall into the hands of the living God.

Hebrews 10: 26 – 31

THE ROOM

The deep dark secret place in a man's soul; from where the motivations arise to potentially commit transgressions against Divine Law that he would rather not divulge to any other man; is the same place he can find the One that can free him from his slavery to the thoughts that bind him.

Jesus said: "And when you pray, do not imitate the hypocrites: they love to say their prayers standing in the synagogues and at street corners for people to see them. I tell you solemnly, they have had their reward. But when you pray, go to your private room and when you have shut the door, pray to your Father who is in that secret place, and your Father who sees all that is done in secret will reward you." Matthew 6:5-6

The path to peace and freedom which is "steep, windy and hard", starts in that secret place.

Don't be afraid to let Jesus in the door.

THE CHURCH'S ULTIMATE TRIAL

CCC675

Before Christ's second coming, the Church must pass through a final trial that will shake the faith of many believers. The persecution that accompanies her pilgrimage on earth will unveil the "mystery of iniquity" in the form of a religious deception offering men an apparent solution to their problems at the price of apostasy from the truth. The supreme religious deception is that of the Antichrist, a pseudo-messianism by which man glorifies himself in the place of God and of his Messiah come in the flesh.

CCC676

CLAIMS ARE MADE THAT THE MESSIANIC HOPE WILL BE REALISED WITHIN HISTORY. "The Church has rejected even modified forms of this falsification of the kingdom under the name of millenarianism, especially the intrinsically perverse political form of a" SECULAR .MESSIANISM.

MESSIANIC HOPE *CAN ONLY* BE REALISED *BEYOND HISTORY*

CCC677

The Church will enter the glory of the kingdom only through this final Passover, when she will follow her lord in his death and resurrection. The kingdom will be fulfilled, then, not by a historic triumph of the Church through a progressive ascendancy, but only by God's victory over the final unleashing of evil, which will cause her bride to come down from heaven. God's triumph over the revolt of evil will take the form of the LAST JUDGEMENT after the final cosmic upheaval of this passing world.

CCC678   JUDGEMENT OF THE LIVING AND THE DEAD

Following the steps of the prophets and John the Baptist, Jesus announced the judgement of the Last day in His preaching. Then will the conduct of each one, and the secrets of hearts be brought to light. Then will the *culpable* unbelief that countered the offer of God's Grace as nothing, be condemned Our attitude about our neighbour will disclose acceptance or refusal of Grace and Divine Love. On the last day Jesus will say: "Truly I say to you, as you did it to one of the least of my brethren, you did it to me."

CCC679   ETERNAL LIFE

Christ is Lord of Eternal Life. Full right to pass definitive judgement on the works and hearts of men belong to Him as redeemer of the world. He "acquired" this right by His cross. The Father has given "all judgement to the Son". Yet the Son did not come to judge, but to save and to give the life He has in Himself. By rejecting Grace in this life, one already judges oneself, receives according to ones works, and can even condemn oneself for all eternity by rejecting the Spirit of love.

Note: Definition of Grace in the theological sense (Pocket Oxford Dictionary)
- Favour of God
- Divine regeneration and inspiring influence
- State of being so influenced

St Augustine wrote that Heaven is the eternal now. Therefore, at the hour of death, one is in eternity and Messianic hope *may* be realised.

DELIVER US

Libera nos, quaesumus, Domine, ab omnibus malis, da propitious pacem in diebus nostris, u tope misericordiae tuae adiuti, et a peccato simus simper liberi, et ab amni perturbation secure: expentantes beatum spem et adventum Salvatoris nostril Ieusu Christi.

DELIVER US, LORD, WE BESEECH YOU, FROM EVERY EVIL AND GRANT US PEACE IN OUR DAY, SO THAT AIDED BY YOUR MERCY WE *MIGHT* BE EVER FREE FROM SIN AND PROTECTED FROM ALL ANXIETY, AS WE AWAIT THE BLESSED HOPE AND THE COMING OF OUR SAVIOUR, JESUS CHRIST.

See CCC2850-54.

SORTING IT OUT
(Paraphrasing the Catechism)

If a man pronounces a harsh judgement on another, somewhere down the line he will be judged will the full measure he dealt out himself. That's the way it always goes. That's not to say he can't make a judgement in the context of the common good, he has that right. There is a big difference between tolerance and permissiveness. Also, if you speak the truth, more often than not these days, you will be accused of being "judgemental." Truth and reality can be very stressful concepts for some people.

We are all called as men, to be "Priest, Prophet and King." We are called to sit in judgment of ourselves and our conduct with the help of the Holy Spirit. He convicts and guides us, through the Magisterium of the Catholic Church – Her sacred scripture and Tradition. But, most importantly, with the help of genuine brothers and sisters in Christ.

When a man looks objectively at his own conduct without self-condemnation -which comes from the enemy- and endeavours to maintain a constant state of self examination, repentance and on-going conversion he will gradually achieve more and more freedom from the chains of slavery to sin.

The peace Jesus promises will start to become a reality and this peace is one the world can *never* give or take away. Along with that comes freedom from fear and anxiety which will be replaced with steadfast courage and also a kind of loyalty to God and family that can't be shaken. In short – don't look over the fence, sort your own stuff out.

Sean O'Tuathail
31 March 2009

FREEDOM OR FREE DOOM?

CCC1731
Freedom is the power, rooted in reason and will, to act or not to act, to do this or that, and so to perform deliberate actions on one's *own* responsibility. By *Free will* one shapes one's own life. Human freedom is a force for growth and maturity in truth and goodness; it attains its perfection when directed toward God, our beatitude.

CCC1732
As long as freedom has not bound itself definitively to its ultimate good which is God, there is a possibility of CHOOSING BETWEEN GOOD AND EVIL, and thus of growing in perfection or of failing and sinning. This freedom characterizes properly human acts. It is the basis or praise or blame, merit or reproach.

CCC1733
The more one does what is good, the *freer one becomes*. There is no true freedom expect the service of what is good and just. THE CHOICE TO DISOBEY AND DO EVIL IS AN ABUSE OF FREEDOM AND LEADS TO "THE SLAVERY OF SIN."

CCC1734
Freedom makes man responsible for his acts to the extent that they are voluntary. Progress in Virtue, knowledge of the good, and ascesis (self-discipline) enhance the mastery of the will over its acts.

CCC1735
Immutability (Attributability) and responsibility for an action can be diminished or even nullified by ignorance, inadvertence, duress, fear, habit, inordinate attachments, and other psychological or social factors.

CCC1736
Every ACT directly WILLED is imputable to its author...

HE TOOK IT ALL ON.
Hebrews 10: 11-18

All the (O.T) priests stand at their duties every day, offering over and over again the same sacrifices which are quite incapable of taking sins away. Jesus, on the other hand, has offered *one single sacrifice for his sins* and then taken his place forever, at the right hand of God, where he is now waiting until his enemies are made into a footstool for him. By virtue of that one single offering, he was achieved the eternal perfection of all who he is sanctifying. The Holy Spirit assures us of this; for he says, first:

> This is the Covenant I will make with
> them when those days arrive;

> Jeremiah: 31

> And the Lord then goes on to say:
> I will put my laws into their hearts
> and write them on their minds.
> I will never call their sins to mind
> or their offences.
> When all sins are forgiven, there can be no more sin offerings.

Note, The Mass RE-PRESENTS the once and for all sacrifice Jesus made – it does not "re-sacrifice Jesus" as some mistakenly claim.

MARK 7:20-23

And he went on, 'It is what comes out of a man that makes him unclean, for it is from within, from men's hearts, that evil intentions emerge: fornication, theft, murder, adultery, avarice, malice, deceit, indecency, envy, slander, pride, folly. All these evil things come from within and make a man unclean.'

www.ingramcontent.com/pod-product-compliance
Lightning Source LLC
Chambersburg PA
CBHW082335300426
44109CB00046B/2484